stories for the extreme teen's heart

Books in the Stories for the Heart Collection

Stories for a Teen's Heart, Book 1

Stories for a Teen's Heart, Book 2

Stories for the Extreme Teen's Heart

Journal for a Teen's Heart

Stories for the Heart, The Second Collection
(Previously published as More Stories for the Heart)

Stories for the Family's Heart

Stories for a Woman's Heart

Stories for a Man's Heart

Stories for a Faithful Heart

Stories for a Mom's Heart

Stories for a Dad's Heart

Stories for a Kindred Heart

Stories for a Cheerful Heart

Christmas Stories for the Heart

Stories for a Grad's Heart

Books by Alice Gray in the Multnomah Gift Line

The Fragrance of Friendship

A Pleasant Place

Morning Coffee and Time Alone

Quiet Moments and a Cup of Tea

Gentle Is a Grandmother's Love

Once upon a Christmas

what teens are saying about this book

A great collection of inspiring stories that will remain engraved on your heart. This book *shows* that we as teens can persevere and rise above the pressures and problems in our lives. These are enduring stories that will challenge you, restore your hope, make you smile, and lift your spirits again and again.

Shanna Stroebel
Age 16

This book is something I know I can come to for encouragement, inspiration, or just to put a smile on my face. There was at least one story for almost every situation in my life. This book is perfect for those who want to be reminded of how awesome God is. I loved reading it!

Kristen Lamoreaux
Age 14

Stories for the Extreme Teen's Heart is an excellent compilation of short stories that will set a spark in hearts for God and get teens yearning after Him. Each story impacted me in a different way, yet all led me to thinking about how God has worked miraculously in my own life.

Nathan Livsey
Age 18

I think this is an awesome book. It has encouraged me, making me smile and laugh. It doesn't matter where you read, all of the stories are great. No matter who you are, I think you'll find some you can relate to yourself. I recommend *Stories for the Extreme Teen's Heart* for my friends and other teenagers, too.

Danae Jacobson
Age 15

This book is for any teenager who wants to live a sold-out and radical Christian life. It gives us stories of extreme faith, living for God, standing up for what we believe, and making unselfish choices in a selfish world. This is just what teens need to read!

Rachel Neet
Age 15

This book is good for a lot of reasons—one reason is the incredible selection of stories. Some make you laugh, some lift your spirits, and some leave you with the realization that God always works in whatever situation you are in. I hope there is a sequel!

Jeremy Morris
Age 15

Stories for the Extreme Teen's Heart is a truly inspirational book. After reading these stories, I find myself wanting to become a radical, on-fire-for-God teen. It has encouraged me to press on harder in my relationship with Jesus Christ.

This book has shown me the true meaning of "Jesus Freak"—and now I want to be one.

Danielle Strannigan
Age 16

I'm really glad I had a chance to read these stories, because I enjoyed every one of them. I liked how they compared to situations in my own life. It's a great idea that other young adults will have a chance to read these stories—it can help them like it helped me. Thanks a lot!

Fabian Clark
Age 17

This book is great! It deals with all phases of life—ups and downs. The stories left me inspired, encouraged, smiling, and even convicted. Some of today's messages for teens are so discouraging, making them feel worthless and like life has no meaning; but this book is very encouraging with the message that life is very worthwhile and that you have a purpose, no matter what comes your way.

Sarah McGhehey
Age 17

Many stories in this book have brought me to tears and that have really made me think about my life. It's full of real people, real situations, and real victories. This is just the thing for teenagers who want to live an extreme life for God. I strongly endorse this book.

Nathan Neet
Age 17

I really loved reading these stories for teens. They reminded me of things that have happened in my own life and made me ask myself, *What would Jesus do in this situation?* I think kids are going to love this book!

Amy Carmichael
Age 19

This book opened my eyes to a lot of things—like how a bitter person can change with the love of God. It also made me stop and think about how fortunate I am to know the love of God, and it caused me to want to share that love with those around me. I encourage anyone—Christian and non-Christian—to read these inspirational stories.

Lily Clark
Age 16

I was struggling with a spiritual issue in my life and these stories helped me to see that I needed to live my life fully for God. Hopefully, if other teens are going through something in their lives, they can sit down with this book and get a new understanding of what God desires for them.

Monica Bethel
Age 15

stories for the extreme teen's heart

COMPILED BY ALICE GRAY

Multnomah® Publishers *Sisters, Oregon*

STORIES FOR THE EXTREME TEEN'S HEART
published by Multnomah Publishers, Inc.

© 2000 by Multnomah Publishers, Inc.
International Standard Book Number: 1-57673-703-9 (Paperback)

International Standard Book Number: 1-57673-783-7 (Paperback with CD)

Cover photograph inside oval by David Bailey Photography
Interior photography by David Bailey Photography and Multnomah
Image on spine by Photodisc
Cartoons by Chaz Chapman from Interior Illustrations
www.chazchapman.com

Scriptures are taken from: *The Holy Bible,* New International Version (NIV)
© 1973, 1984 by International Bible Society,
used by permission of Zondervan Publishing House.

Holy Bible, New Living Translation (NLT) © 1996.
Used by permission of Tyndale House Publishers, Inc. All rights reserved.

The Message © 1993 by Eugene H. Peterson.

Multnomah is a trademark of Multnomah Publishers, Inc.,
and is registered in the U.S. Patent and Trademark Office.
The colophon is a trademark of Multnomah Publishers, Inc.

Stories for the Heart is a trademark of Multnomah Publishers, Inc.
and is registered in the U.S. Patent and Trademark Office.

Printed in the United States of America

01 02 03 04 05 06—11 12 10 9 8 7 6 5 4

A time to remember and a time to hope

Remembering teens who gave their lives for God...

You are today's inspiration.

Celebrating teens who are living for God...

You are tomorrow's hope.

aspecialthankyou

The authors
for writing stories that honor teens.

Chaz Chapman
for capturing life in cartoon art.

Steve Gardner
for extraordinary cover and interior design.

Jennifer Gates, Teri Sharp, and Shawn Strannigan
*for research, permissions, manuscript preparation
and a hundred other details that make words into a book.*

Doreen Button, Sheila Miller, Lenette Stroebel,
Sauna Winsor, and Casandra Lindell
for helping us find extraordinary stories.

Monica Bethel, Amy Carmichael,
Fabian Clark, Lily Clark, Danae Jacobson,
Kristen Lamoreaux, Nathan Livsey, Sarah McGhehey,
Jeremy Morris, Nathan Neet, Rachel Neet,
Danielle Strannigan, *and* Shanna Stroebel
*for helping us select the "best of the best" stories.
Your teen perspective and enthusiastic
comments were our inspiration.*

contentscontentscontents

forgiveness

virtue

sharing your faith

making a difference

inspiration

trust and courage

changed lives

faith

forgiveness

regret

He that cannot forgive others,
breaks the bridge over which he himself must pass…

GEORGE HERBERT

Friends to the End

CYNTHIA HAMOND

f riends to the end!" Breana had signed the picture of us that hung on my bedroom wall. We were so happy the night it was taken, all confidence and smiles.

Breana's handwritten promise looped and curled with the joy we had shared. "Friends to the end," and I was the one who ended it.

We had been friends for ten years, since the day I'd moved next door the summer before second grade. I was standing on the sidewalk watching the moving van being unloaded and then, there was Breana, straddling her bike beside me.

"That your bike?" She pointed at the pink bike my father was wheeling into the garage.

"Yes."

"Wanna ride to the park?"

"Sure."

Just that simply, we became friends. More really. We were next-door sisters.

Maybe if I could look back and say, "that is the moment our friendship ended," I could repair it. But there wasn't a dramatic split. I made one choice, one step, one rip at a time, until I had walked away from Breana and into my new life with my new friends.

I guess I could really say that Breana started it. It was her idea for me to try out for cheerleading. "You're the best dancer in our class and the best gymnast in the club. You'd be a natural."

"You're crazy." I protested, though I really did believe her and I did want to try out. I knew that Breana knew that. It was her job to talk me into it, then if I failed, it would have been all her idea and I could shrug it off with a "what did I tell you?"

I finally gave in when Breana promised to try out with me. She went to all the practices, learned the routines, and spent two weeks in the backyard coaching me.

Breana was as excited as I was when I made the squad and more surprised than I was when she did too.

The night of our first football game, Breana gave me a cross necklace that matched the one she had on. "To remind us that Jesus is the One who deserves our cheers and all the glory," she said.

Our halftime performance was flawless, even the grand-finale lift. I jumped into my stance with Breana beneath me as my secure base. I posed on her shoulders and smiled for the flash of my father's camera.

It was this picture of us that Breana had signed.

One afternoon after football practice, Drew Paterson caught up with us and asked me to the Homecoming Dance. My brain didn't know how to talk to Drew Paterson. I could only nod. His blues eyes alone were enough to leave me speechless.

Breana was the one who finally answered, "She'd love to!"

The night of the dance, Breana helped me do my hair and makeup and then left me with a hug. "Look for the heart. I'll be waiting up."

The heart. We had made those hearts for each other so many Valentine's Days ago that I don't remember when we started hanging them in our bedroom windows as a signal to meet at the back porch swing.

I shared everything with Breana after the first, second, and even third date. After that, I began to make up excuses. It was too late, or I was too tired. It wasn't like I was doing anything really wrong. It was just that I knew Breana wouldn't understand the kinds of parties I was going to and the people I was with. Why did I have to explain myself to her anyway?

That stupid heart began to anger me. "Just grow up, Breana," I'd spit under my breath when I passed by her window after a night out with Drew.

Until last night, when I didn't just pass by her window but nearly passed out under it. I was losing my balance and then there was Breana, cradling my head in her lap, her cross pendant shining in the moonlight between us. Seeing it reminded me of who I was and who I belonged to. I reached up to touch where mine used to hang. How long had it been since I had thought to wear it?

Breana brushed my hair back out of my eyes.

"You are the real Miss Goody Two-shoes," I said and burst into tears.

That's what Drew had called me at the party. "A toast to Miss Goody Two-shoes. She's too good to drink with the rest of us sinners," he had said loud enough for everyone to hear.

My new friends lifted their drinks in mock salute. "To Saint Jeanine."

I laughed the hollow laugh that I had heard myself use so often the last four weeks. Then I grabbed Drew's drink and gulped it down. They all hooted their approval.

The alcohol's harshness shocked me. I couldn't breathe and when I finally gasped in air, I went into a coughing spasm. My stomach rolled. I needed help. I grabbed for Drew but he dodged my reach.

"I guess some people just can't handle their liquor." He pointed at me and they all snickered. Standing in the center of their ridicule, I suddenly wanted nothing more than to be the person they were accusing me of being.

These were my new friends? They laughed *with* me if I did what they did but *at* me if I didn't.

"Please, Drew, I want to go home."

"Sure thing," he said, much to my relief. He wasn't such a bad guy. Tomorrow I would talk to him. I knew I could make him understand about his friends and these parties. After all, he had said that he loved me.

Drew took my hand and led me out the door to the sidewalk. He turned me towards home. "Go play with your dolls. Call me when you grow up."

I stumbled the six blocks to home. It wasn't until I saw the heart in Breana's window that I knew I had made it. I had made it back to home and back to myself.

The next morning came fresh and new but just a little too early for me.

I struggled out of bed and cleaned up for the day. This time I didn't forget to put on my cross. Faith renewed, I fastened the chain with a sense of joy. I was starting over.

I flung open my curtains and hung my old Valentine's heart in the window. I wanted it to be the first thing Breana saw this morning. I could hardly wait for our reunion on the back porch swing, to be together again.

Looking across at her bedroom, I almost expected to see Breana smiling over at me. The last thing I expected to see is what I saw. The heart was gone. Her window was empty.

I walked through the house and out to our swing in a fog of shock. There the shock turned to pain. On the swing cushion was half of the heart from her window. Breana had written just two words, *The End.*

I sank into the swing as torn apart as the heart I held on my lap. The faded heart turned deep red where my tears dropped on it. I reached up and touched my cross. It had taken me too long to see the truth. I was too late.

"I see you're wearing your cross again." I looked up at Breana standing over me. I wiped my tears and nodded.

"Jeanine, you know that Jesus restores the brokenhearted."

"Yes, Breana, I believe that."

Breana sat down. She placed the other half of the heart beside the one in my lap. On it were the words *Friends To.*

I studied the pieced-together heart for a moment before grasping what it meant. Hope started to fill me and I began to cry.

"Friends to the end?" I finally managed to ask.

"Yes," Breana smiled and gave the swing a little push start with her foot. "Friends to the end."

Wounds from a friend are better than many kisses from an enemy.

PROVERBS 27:6
NEW LIVING TRANSLATION

I Will Always Forgive You

JONI EARECKSON TADA
FROM *TELL ME THE PROMISES*

Lisa sat on the floor of her old room, staring at the box that lay in front of her. It was an old shoe box that she had decorated to become a memory box many years before. Stickers and penciled flowers covered the top and sides. Its edges were worn, the corners of the lid taped so as to keep their shape.

It had been three years since Lisa last opened the box. A sudden move to Boston had kept her from packing it. But now that she was back home, she took the time to look again at the memories.

Fingering the corners of the box and stroking its cover, Lisa pictured in her mind what was inside.

There was a photo of the family trip to the Grand Canyon, a note from her friend telling her that Nick Bicotti liked her, and the Indian arrowhead she had found while on her senior class trip.

One by one, she remembered the items in the box, lingering over the sweetest, until she came to the last and only painful memory. She knew what it looked like—a single sheet of paper upon which lines had been drawn to form boxes, 490 of them to be exact. And each box contained a check mark, one for each time.

"How many times must I forgive my brother?" the disciple Peter had asked Jesus. "Seven times?" Lisa's Sunday school teacher had read Jesus' surprise answer to the class. "Seventy times seven."

Lisa had leaned over to her brother Brent as the teacher continued reading. "How many times is that?" she whispered. Brent, though two years younger, was smarter than she was.

"Four hundred and ninety," Brent wrote on the corner of his Sunday school paper. Lisa saw the message, nodded, and sat back in her chair. She watched her brother as the lesson continued. He was small for his age, with narrow shoulders and short arms. His glasses were too large for his face, and his hair always matted in swirls. He bordered on being a nerd, but his incredible skills at everything, especially music, made him popular with his classmates.

Brent had learned to play the piano at age four, the clarinet at age seven, and had just begun to play oboe. His music teachers said he'd be a famous musician someday. There was only one thing at which Lisa was better at than Brent—basketball. They played it almost every afternoon after school. Brent could have refused to play, but he knew that it was Lisa's only joy in the midst of her struggles to get C's and D's at school.

Lisa's attention came back to her Sunday school teacher as the woman finished the lesson and closed with prayer. That same Sunday afternoon found brother and sister playing basketball in the driveway. It was then that the counting had begun. Brent was guarding Lisa as she dribbled toward the basket. He had tried to bat the ball away, got his face near her elbow, and took a shot on the chin. "Ow!" he cried out and turned away.

Lisa saw her opening and drove to the basket, making an easy layup. She gloated over her success but stopped when she saw Brent. "You okay?" she asked. Brent shrugged his shoulders.

"Sorry," Lisa said. "Really. It was a cheap shot."

"It's all right. I forgive you," he said. A thin smile then formed on his face. "Just 489 more times though."

"Whaddaya mean?" Lisa asked.

"You know…what we learned in Sunday school today. You're supposed to forgive someone 490 times. I just forgave you, so now you have 489 left," he kidded. The two of them laughed at the thought of keeping track of every time Lisa had done something to Brent. They were sure she had gone past 490 long ago.

The rain interrupted their game, and the two moved indoors.

"Wanna play Battleship?" Lisa asked. Brent agreed, and they were soon on the floor of the living room with their game boards in front of them. Each took turns calling out a letter and number combination, hoping to hit each other's ships.

Lisa knew she was in trouble as the game went on. Brent had only lost one ship out of five. Lisa had lost three. Desperate to win, she found herself leaning over the edge of Brent's barrier ever so slightly. She was thus able to see where Brent had placed two of his ships. She quickly evened the score.

Pleased, Lisa searched once more for the location of the last two ships. She peered over the barrier again, but this time Brent caught her in the act. "Hey, you're cheating!" he stared at her in disbelief.

Lisa's face turned red. Her lips quivered. "I'm sorry," she said, staring at the carpet. There was not much Brent could say. He knew Lisa sometimes did things like this. He felt sorry that Lisa found so few things she could do well. It was wrong for her to cheat, but he knew the temptation was hard for her.

"Okay, I forgive you," Brent said. Then he added with a small laugh, "I guess it's down to 488 now, huh?"

"Yeah, I guess so." She returned his kindness with a weak smile and added, "Thanks for being my brother, Brent."

Brent's forgiving spirit gripped Lisa, and she wanted him to know how sorry she was. It was that evening that she had made the chart with the 490 boxes. She showed it to him before he went to bed.

"We can keep track of every time I mess up and you forgive me," she said. "See, I'll put a check in each box—like this." She placed two marks in the upper left-hand boxes.

"These are for today."

Brent raised his hands to protest. "You don't need to keep—"

"Yes, I do!" Lisa interrupted. "You're always forgiving me, and I want to keep track. Just let me do this!" She went back to her room and tacked the chart to her bulletin board.

There were many opportunities to fill in the chart in the years that followed. She once told the kids at school that Brent talked in his sleep and called out Rhonda Hill's name, even though it wasn't true. The teasing caused Brent days and days of misery. When she realized how cruel she had been, Lisa apologized sincerely. That night she marked box number 98. Forgiveness number 211 came in the tenth grade when Lisa failed to bring home his English book. Brent had stayed home sick that day and had asked her to bring it so he could study for a quiz. She forgot and he got a C.

Number 393 was for lost keys...418 for the extra bleach she put in the washer, which ruined his favorite polo shirt...449, the dent she had put in his car when she had borrowed it.

There was a small ceremony when Lisa checked number 490. She used a gold pen for the check mark, had Brent sign the chart, and then placed it in her memory box.

"I guess that's the end," Lisa said. "No more screw-ups from me anymore!"

Brent just laughed. "Yeah, right."

Number 491 was just another one of Lisa's careless mistakes, but its hurt lasted a lifetime. Brent had become all that his music teachers said he would. Few could play the oboe better than he. In his fourth year at the best music school in the United States, he received the opportunity of a lifetime—a chance to try out for New York City's great orchestra.

The tryout would be held sometime during the following two weeks. It would be the fulfillment of his young dreams. But he never got the chance. Brent had been out when the call about the tryout came to the house.

Lisa was the only one home and on her way out the door, eager to get to work on time.

"Two-thirty on the tenth," the secretary said on the phone. Lisa did not have a pen, but she told herself that she could remember it.

"Got it. Thanks." I can remember that, she thought. But she did not.

It was a week later around the dinner table that Lisa realized her mistake.

"So, Brent," his mom asked him, "When do you try out?"

"Don't know yet. They're supposed to call." Lisa froze in her seat.

"Oh, no!" she blurted out loud. "What's today's date? Quick!"

"It's the twelfth," her dad answered. "Why?"

A terrible pain ripped through Lisa's heart. She buried her face in her hands, crying. "Lisa, what's the matter?" her mother asked.

Through sobs, Lisa explained what had happened. "It was two days ago… the tryout…two-thirty…the call came… last week." Brent sat back in his chair, not believing Lisa.

"Is this one of your jokes, sis?" he asked, though he could tell her misery was real. She shook her head, still unable to look at him.

"Then I really missed it?" She nodded.

Brent ran out of the kitchen without a word. He did not come out of his room the rest of the evening. Lisa tried once to knock on the door, but she could not face him. She went to her room where she cried bitterly.

Suddenly she knew what she had to do. She had ruined Brent's life. He could never forgive her for that. She had failed her family, and there was nothing to do but to leave home. Lisa packed her pickup truck in the middle of the night and left a note behind, telling her folks she'd be all right. She began writing a note to Brent, but her words sounded empty to her. Nothing I say could make a difference anyway, she thought.

Two days later she got a job as a waitress in Boston. She found an apartment not too far from the restaurant. Her parents tried many times to reach her, but Lisa ignored their letters.

"It's too late," she wrote them once. "I've ruined Brent's life, and I'm not coming back."

Lisa did not think she would ever see home again. But one day in the restaurant where she worked she saw a face she knew: "Lisa!" said Mrs. Nelson, looking up from her plate. "What a surprise."

The woman was a friend of Lisa's family from back home. "I was so sorry to hear about your brother," Mrs. Nelson said softly. "Such a terrible accident. But we can be thankful that he died quickly. He didn't suffer." Lisa stared at the woman in shock.

"Wh-hat," she finally stammered.

It couldn't be! Her brother? Dead? The woman quickly saw that Lisa did not know about the accident. She told the girl the sad story of the speeding car, the rush to the hospital, the doctors working over Brent. But all they could do was not enough to save him.

Lisa returned home that afternoon.

Now she found herself in her room thinking about her brother as she held the small box that held some of her memories of him. Sadly, she opened the box and peered inside. It was as she remembered, except for one item—Brent's chart. It was not there. In its place, at the bottom of the box, was an envelope. Her hands shook as she tore it open and removed a letter.

The first page read:

Dear Lisa,

It was you who kept count, not me. But if you're stubborn enough to keep count, use the new chart I've made for you.

Love,
Brent

Lisa turned to the second page where she found a chart just like the one she had made as a child, but on this one the lines were drawn in perfect precision. And unlike the chart she had kept, there was but one check mark in the upper left-hand corner. Written in red felt-tip pen over the entire page were the words: "Number 491. Forgiven, forever."

At that point Peter got up the nerve to ask,
"Master, how many times do I forgive
a brother or sister who hurts me? Seven?"
Jesus replied, "Seven! Hardly. Try seventy times seven."

MATTHEW 18:21–22
THE MESSAGE

Washed Away

JANIS M. WHIPPLE

I t was a cold, gray January morning. I'd gone to the beach to walk. I had a lot on my mind, and I wanted to be alone. I wanted to feel close to God again.

As I walked, I picked up a stick and wrote in the sand. I named four things that had hurt me and disappointed God. And I wrote the word peace, which I wanted, but did not have. I dropped the stick and kept going. As I walked, I prayed, crying on God's shoulder.

When I noticed the tide coming in, I turned back. I looked for the words I had written. The stick was there, but the water had washed away all the words except one: peace. God had washed away my pain and left a promise of peace.

The Room

JOSHUA HARRIS

FROM *I KISSED DATING GOODBYE*

In that place between wakefulness and dreams, I found myself in the room. There were no distinguishing features save for the one wall covered with small index-card files. They were the ones in libraries that list titles by author or subject in alphabetical order. But these files, which stretched from floor to ceiling and seemingly endless in either direction, had very different headings. As I drew near the wall of files, the first to catch my attention was one that read "Girls I Have Liked." I opened it and began flipping through the cards. I quickly shut it, shocked to realize that I recognized the names written on each one.

And then without being told, I knew exactly where I was. This lifeless room with its small files was a crude catalog system for my life. Here were written the actions of my every moment, big and small, in a detail my memory couldn't match.

A sense of wonder and curiosity, coupled with horror, stirred within me as I began randomly opening files and exploring their contents. Some brought joy and sweet memories; others a sense of shame and regret so intense that I would look over my shoulder to see if anyone was watching. A file named "Friends" was next to one marked "Friends I Have Betrayed."

The titles ranged from the mundane to the outright weird. "Books I Have Read," "Lies I Have Told," "Comfort I Have Given," "Jokes I Have Laughed At." Some were almost hilarious in their exactness: "Things I've Yelled at My Brothers." Others I couldn't laugh at: "Things I Have Done in

Anger," "Things I Have Muttered under My Breath at My Parents." I never ceased to be surprised by the contents. Often there were many more cards than I expected. Sometimes there were fewer than I hoped.

I was overwhelmed by the sheer volume of the life I had lived. Could it be possible that I had the time in my twenty years to write each of these thousands, possibly millions, of cards? But each card confirmed this truth. Each was written in my own handwriting. Each signed with my signature.

When I pulled out the file marked "Songs I Have Listened To," I realized the files grew to contain their contents. The cards were packed tightly, and yet after two or three yards, I hadn't found the end of the file. I shut it, shamed, not so much by the quality of music, but more by the vast amount of time I knew that file represented.

When I came to a file marked "Lustful Thoughts," I felt a chill run through my body. I pulled the file out only an inch, not willing to test its size, and drew out a card. I shuddered at its detailed contents. I felt sick to think that such a moment had been recorded.

Suddenly I felt an almost animal rage. One thought dominated my mind: "No one must ever see these cards! No one must ever see this room! I have to destroy them!" In an instant frenzy I yanked the file out. Its size didn't matter now. I had to empty it and burn the cards. But as I took the file at one end and began pounding it on the floor, I could not dislodge a single card. I became desperate and pulled out a card, only to find it as strong as steel when I tried to tear it.

Defeated and utterly helpless, I returned the file to its slot. Leaning my forehead against the wall, I let out a long, self-pitying sigh. And then I saw it. The title bore "People I Have Shared the Gospel With." The handle was brighter than those around it, newer, almost unused. I pulled on its handle and a small box not more than three inches long fell into my hands. I could count the cards it contained on one hand.

And then the tears came. I began to weep. Sobs so deep that the hurt started in my stomach and shook through me. I fell on my knees and cried. I cried out of shame, from the overwhelming shame of it all. The rows of file shelves swirled in my tear-filled eyes. No one must ever, ever know of this room. I must lock it up and hide the key.

But then as I pushed away the tears, I saw Him. No, please not Him. Not here. Oh, anyone but Jesus.

I watched helplessly as He began to open the files and read the cards. I couldn't bear to watch His response. And in the moments I could bring myself to look at His face, I saw a sorrow deeper than my own. He seemed to intuitively go to the worst boxes. Why did He have to read every one?

Finally He turned and looked at me from across the room. He looked at me with pity in His eyes. But this was a pity that didn't anger me. I dropped my head, covered my face with my hands and began to cry again. He walked over and put His arm around me. He could have said so many things. But He didn't say a word. He just cried with me.

Then He got up and walked back to the wall of files. Starting at one end of the room, He took out a file and, one by one, began to sign His name over mine on each card.

"No!" I shouted, rushing to Him. All I could find to say was "No, no," as I pulled the card from Him. His name shouldn't be on these cards. But there it was, written in red so rich, so dark, so alive. The name of Jesus covered mine. It was written with His blood.

He gently took the card back. He smiled a sad smile and continued to sign the cards. I don't think I'll ever understand how He did it so quickly, but the next instant it seemed I heard Him close the last file and walk back to my side. He placed His hand on my shoulder and said, "It is finished."

I stood up, and He led me out of the room. There was no lock on its door. There were still cards to be written.

But if we confess our sins to him, he is faithful and just
to forgive us and cleanse us from every wrong.

1 JOHN 1:9
NEW LIVING TRANSLATION

The Lovesick Father

PHILIP YANCEY
FROM *WHAT'S SO AMAZING ABOUT GRACE?*

young girl grows up on a cherry orchard just above Traverse City, Michigan. Her parents, a bit old fashioned, tend to overreact to her nose ring, the music she listens to, and the length of her skirts. They ground her a few times, and she seethes inside. "I hate you!" she screams at her father when he knocks on the door of her room after an argument, and that night she acts on a plan she has mentally rehearsed scores of times. She runs away.

She has visited Detroit only once before, on a bus trip with her church youth group to watch the Tigers play. Because newspapers in Traverse City report in lurid details the gangs, the drugs, and the violence in downtown Detroit, she concludes that this is probably the last place her parents will look for her. California, maybe, or Florida, but not Detroit.

Her second day there she meets a man who drives the biggest car she's ever seen. He offers her a ride, buys her lunch, arranges a place for her to stay. He gives her some pills that make her feel better than she's ever felt before. She was right all along, she decides: her parents were keeping her from all the fun.

The good life continues for a month, two months, a year. The man with the big car—she calls him "Boss"—teaches her a few things that men like. Since she's underage, men pay a premium for her. She lives in a penthouse, and orders room service whenever she wants. Occasionally she thinks about the folks back home, but their lives now seem so boring and provincial that she can hardly believe she grew up there.

She has a brief scare when she sees her picture printed on the back of a milk carton with the headline "Have you seen this child?" But by now she has blond hair, and with all the makeup and body-piercing jewelry she wears, nobody would mistake her for a child. Besides, most of her friends are runaways, and nobody squeals in Detroit.

After a year the first sallow signs of illness appear, and it amazes her how fast the boss turns mean. "These days, we can't mess around," he growls, and before she knows it she's out on the street without a penny to her name. She still turns a couple of tricks a night, but they don't pay much, and all the money goes to support her habit. When winter blows in she finds herself sleeping on metal grates outside the big department stores. "Sleeping" is the wrong word—a teenage girl at night in downtown Detroit can never relax her guard. Dark bands circle her eyes. Her cough worsens.

One night as she lies awake listening for footsteps, all of a sudden everything about her life looks different. She no longer feels like a woman of the world. She feels like a little girl, lost in a cold and frightening city. She begins to whimper. Her pockets are empty and she's hungry. She needs a fix. She pulls legs tight underneath her and shivers under the newspapers she's piled atop her coat. Something jolts a synapse of memory and a single image fills her mind: of May in Traverse City, when a million cherry trees bloom at once, with her golden retriever dashing through the rows and rows of blossomy trees in chase of a tennis ball.

God, why did I leave, she says to herself, and pain stabs at her heart. *My dog back home eats better than I do now.* She's sobbing, and she knows in a flash that more than anything else in the world she wants to go home.

Three straight phone calls, three straight connections with the answering machine. She hangs up without leaving a message the first two times, but the third time she says, "Dad, Mom, it's me. I was wondering about maybe coming home. I'm catching a bus up your way, and it'll get there about midnight tomorrow. If you're not there, well, I guess I'll just stay on the bus until it hits Canada."

It takes about seven hours for a bus to make all the stops between Detroit and Traverse City, and during that time she realizes the flaws in her plan. What if her parents are out of town and miss the message? Shouldn't she have waited another day or so until she could talk to them? And even if they are home, they probably wrote her off as dead long ago. She should have given them some time to overcome the shock.

Her thoughts bounce back and forth between those worries and the speech she is preparing for her father. "Dad, I'm sorry. I know I was wrong. It's not your fault; it's all mine. Dad, can you forgive me?" She says the words over and over, her throat tightening even as she rehearses them. She hasn't apologized to anyone in years.

The bus has been driving with lights on since Bay City. Tiny snowflakes hit the pavement rubbed worn by thousands of tires, and the asphalt steams. She's forgotten how dark it gets at night out here. A deer darts across the road and the bus swerves. Every so often, a billboard. A sign posting the mileage to Traverse City. *Oh, God.*

When the bus finally rolls into the station, its air brakes hissing in protest, the driver announces in a crackly voice over the microphone, "Fifteen minutes, folks. That's all we have here." Fifteen minutes to decide her life. She checks herself in a compact mirror, smoothes her hair, and licks the lipstick off her teeth. She looks at the tobacco stains on her fingertips, and wonders if her parents will notice. If they're here.

She walks into the terminal not knowing what to expect. Not one of the thousand scenes that have played out in her mind prepare her for what she sees. There, in the concrete-walls-and-plastic-chairs bus terminal in Traverse City, Michigan, stands a group of forty brothers and sisters and great-aunts and uncles and cousins and a grandmother and a great-grandmother to boot. They're all wearing goofy party hats and blowing noise-makers, and taped across an entire wall of the terminal is a computer-generated banner that reads "Welcome home!"

Out of the crowd of well-wishers breaks her dad. She stares out through the tears quivering in her eyes like hot mercury and begins the memorized speech, "Dad, I'm sorry. I know…"

He interrupts her. "Hush child. We've got no time for that. No time for apologies. You'll be late for the party. A banquet's waiting for you at home."

But the father wasn't listening....

"Quick. Bring a clean set of clothes and dress him.

Put the family ring on his finger and sandals on his feet....

We're going to have a feast!

We're going to have a wonderful time!

My son is here—given up for dead and now alive!

Given up for lost and now found!"

And they began to have a wonderful time.

LUKE 15:22–24
THE MESSAGE

Fragrance

MARK TWAIN

Forgiveness is the fragrance
the violet sheds
on the heel that has crushed it.

An Undeserved Honor

JAMIE MORRISON

my life was changed between sixth and seventh periods during my final week of high school. No one else noticed the interaction, but it left an impression with me. In that moment, Keniche, a Japanese student who had moved to our country and our school two years earlier, gave me a small present, neatly wrapped.

I was walking in the hallway between classes when I saw Keniche shuffling my way. His head was down, but I could tell his eyes were scanning the approaching students. When he noticed me, he walked towards me with increased purpose and resolve. I prepared to say a quick hello and pass on by as I always did, but this time was different.

He made a slight gesture with his hand, almost reaching for my elbow before pulling back. Instead of the usual nod, Keniche spoke. "Soddy. Scuse me. Someding fah you. You wait please?"

"Yeah, okay," I said, but inside I was already thinking I would prefer to be on my way than to be seen hanging out with Keniche.

Gracefully, he knelt down, opened his backpack, and pulled out the small package. He stood back up and extended the package in my direction. By instinct, I reached out and held the package, but I still did not suspect it was for me. The shifting in my stance matched the shifting of my eyes; back and forth, briefly at Keniche and then down the hall hoping to be released from this moment. As I watched him, however, his nervous smile and eyes beckoned me to open the gift right there in the hallway.

Removing the paper, I uncovered a small hand-painted ceramic Samurai soldier.[1] Pressing his hands together and bowing slightly, he coaxed his eyes to look into mine. He took a deep breath, then spoke slowly, emphasizing each word so that I would understand the significance of this moment. "You ah bess fren. You been berry nice. You ah kine to me. You teach me yah school." Keniche "explained" the Samurai was from Japan and represented honor, compassion, courage, strength, and wisdom.

My shifting feet and eyes rested.

I stood silently, glancing around the hallway before looking back at him. He was still looking at me, smiling. What could I say? "Thank you?" It seemed like the right thing, but I was humbled. The truth was, I had not been a friend at all. His words echoed in my heart, for there was very little warmth or caring deserving this honor. I had been friendly, but I was never his friend.

My friends and I went out regularly. We would get together for movies or miniature golfing. We went to the beach and to restaurants. We would sometimes play games, listen to music, drive around, or go to the mall…anything that teens do. It never occurred to me to invite Keniche. I never went out with Keniche.

My friends and I would gather for school sporting events. We would watch basketball games or endure the chilly fall evenings in support of the football team. I never joined Keniche at these games, though I would often see him there. He usually dressed in school colors and cheered, even though neither football nor basketball were sports he understood. He even seemed to enjoy himself, but he was always alone. I never cheered with Keniche.

My friends and I would eat together at lunchtime. It was often difficult deciding who to sit with. Should I join classroom friends, youth group friends, soccer or tennis teammates? The decision was never easy. Typically, I would inconvenience everyone by joining an already full table. Keniche ate

---

[1] Samurai means "one who serves." Samurai solders were known for loyalty and service.

lunch in the corner of the cafeteria. He was always alone, usually with his face in a book or studying his food. I never joined Keniche or ate a meal with him.

My friends and I would hang out in between classes. We gathered for jokes and gossip. No matter how short the time, we all looked forward to those moments. I never stopped to talk with Keniche, though I can remember being with friends who snickered as he passed because his clothes weren't cool. I did not stick up for him. I just kept quiet. I never hung out with Keniche or encouraged him to join in my group.

I never knew where he lived. I never knew his last name. I didn't know what he liked to do or eat or whether he had brothers or sisters. I didn't know anything about him. Yet he awarded me the Samurai for being his "best friend."

I did nothing except smile and say "Hi, Keniche" whenever I walked by him. Rarely did I say anything more. It made me sad to think that that was the best friendship he experienced in our school. I was undeserving of the Samurai figure, yet he honored me as the most deserving. To him my actions represented honor, compassion, courage, strength, and wisdom.

There are many hard-earned trophies, plaques, and certificates that now lie somewhere packed away in my storage room or basement or attic. But my Samurai trophy remains on my desk. It is a reminder that friendship and caring are true and lasting awards in life.

Keniche thanked me for a friendship I didn't know I had given. I should thank Keniche for a lesson he couldn't know he had given.

When I Was a Prodigal Son

DON HALL
AS TOLD TO NANETTE THORSEN-SNIPES

t seventeen, I found myself sitting in a jail cell wondering how things could have gone so wrong in my life. I didn't know it then, but looking back, I felt a lot like the Prodigal Son in the Bible.

It was two days after Thanksgiving. Clouds were slung low across the sky and pregnant with rain that cold day in 1983. My mom, my stepdad, Jim, and my younger brother and sister had gone to the grocery store. Before they got home, the phone rang and I answered it.

After asking for my mother, the person on the phone said, "Tell her that Benny hanged himself." It felt as though someone stuck me in the gut with a knife. Benny was my father.

"Is he dead?" I asked, holding my breath, hoping it wasn't true. I couldn't cry. But the pain left an empty hole in me because I didn't know him. When the answer came back "Yes," I sat down to absorb what had happened.

A flood of memories came back. It seemed like a rerun of one of those unbelievable, yet true, stories. My own mother had faced my father's rage one weekend—at the business end of a gun. She finally talked him into putting the weapon down. After he went to work, she packed our bags and moved us out. My brother was seven and I was only four, but I vividly remember being in that motel room where we hid for a week. I had on my cowboy outfit that day, and Mom was crying.

Maybe that's one reason why I stayed angry all those years. I was angry at my father for trying to hurt Mom. Later, I was angry because he died before I could get to know him.

Nothing ever went right for me after my dad died. I couldn't concentrate or learn. I finally quit school in the tenth grade. I went to work as a roofer, carpet cleaner, or anything to earn money.

My anger grew. There were days I made life miserable for Mom and Jim by drinking. But the alcohol brought on more anger, which caused me to lose my temper a lot. I would put my fist through the living room wall or kick in the bathroom door. I was arrested several times for driving under the influence.

One day, I became angry because the bike I'd bought with my hard-earned money wouldn't work right. I picked the ten-speed cycle up over my head and began screaming obscenities. I slammed it repeatedly into the ground until it lay in a crumpled heap.

Mom and Jim became alarmed at my uncontrollable rage and took me to see a counselor, but I didn't want to talk with him. I just sat there and waited for him to quit speaking. After the third session, he gave up and told Mom he couldn't help me if I wouldn't communicate, which suited me just fine.

My drinking worsened, and I had bouts with depression, staying in bed for days. I also started hanging out with bad company and earned myself some dangerous enemies. One day a bullet hit my car as I drove down the highway. I think it was some kids from a rival school. When someone kicked down the basement door where my bedroom was, I, too, became alarmed. I guess that's why I took the gun from my parents' closet that day. I never kept it loaded, but its presence made me feel safe.

The next evening I drove to the hotel where my brother worked. After parking my car, I went straight toward the bar.

Inside, a strong, burly man said, "Son, I need to see your ID." Because I didn't have one, I tried to muscle my way past the guy. He become angry and shoved me. I shoved back. The next thing I knew he smacked me in the jaw, and I hit the floor. I jumped up, waving the gun in his face. Someone had already called the police and in a split second I heard, "Freeze!" I turned to my left where three policemen stood in a firing stance, their guns drawn and aimed directly at me. To my right, I looked down the barrel of another officer's pistol. The scene was chaotic. The police were shouting, "Drop your weapon—Get your hands up on the wall!"

I stood frozen in time. Then an inner voice gently prompted me to go to the wall. I did and was handcuffed and taken to jail.

So for the fourth time, I sat in the county jail with the stench of bodily fluids and sweaty men surrounding me. I didn't worry. Whenever I was caught driving under the influence of alcohol, my parents always posted bail for me. I was shocked when I called for them to get me out and Mom said no.

I didn't realize at the time that they had been on their knees in prayer for me. Finally, they let go and entrusted me to God. Meanwhile, all I could see were the bars on that jail cell and no way out. I knew I was in trouble, and I said a simple prayer: "God, please help me. All I want is a decent life."

A few days later, a friend and his father posted bail for me. Angrily, I went home and packed my things, never once speaking to my parents. Then I moved in with my friend. One night another friend from church dropped by, and through our conversation, I ended up asking Christ into my heart.

Within a year, I met a beautiful young woman named Jennifer at the store where I worked. We later married and now have two great children. In fact, I have spent many evenings witnessing to men in state prisons in Alabama—where I easily could have ended up.

I still regret all the pain I've caused my parents. One recent Christmas, Jim and I went to the grocery store for my mother. While in the cab of the truck, with music softly playing in the background, I said, "Jim, can you ever forgive me for all the pain I put you through?"

The man I knew as my dad looked at me and smiled. "I've already forgiven you, Donnie," he said. Then he put his arm around me. I couldn't help thinking of the story of the Prodigal Son in the Bible and how our heavenly Father always welcomes us home, too.

And while he was still a long distance away, his father saw him coming.
Filled with love and compassion, he ran to his son, embraced him, and kissed him.

LUKE 15:20
NEW LIVING TRANSLATION

Paid in Full

AUTHOR UNKNOWN

after living a "decent" life my time on earth came to an end. The first thing I remember is sitting on a bench in the waiting room of what I thought to be a courthouse. The doors opened, and I was instructed to come in and have a seat by the defense table.

As I looked around I saw the "prosecutor"—he was a villainous-looking gent who snarled as he stared at me. He definitely was the most evil person I have ever seen.

I sat down and looked to my left and there sat my lawyer, a kind and gentle looking man whose appearance seemed very familiar to me. The corner door flew open and there appeared the Judge in full, flowing robes. He commanded an awesome presence as he moved across the room, and I couldn't take my eyes off of him. As he took his seat behind the bench he said, "Let us begin."

The prosecutor rose and said, "My name is Satan, and I am here to show you why this man belongs in hell." He proceeded to tell of lies that I had told, things that I had stolen, and how I had cheated others in the past. Satan told of other horrible perversions that were once in my life, and the more he spoke the further down in my seat I sank. I was so embarrassed that I couldn't look at anyone, even my own lawyer, as the devil told of sins that even I had completely forgotten about.

As upset as I was at Satan for telling all these things about me, I was equally upset at my representative who sat there silently not offering any form of defense at all. I knew I was guilty of those things, but I had done some good in my life—couldn't that at least equal out part of the harm I'd done.

Satan finished with a fury and said, "This man belongs in hell; he is guilty of all that I have charged; and there is not a person who can prove otherwise. Justice will finally be served this day."

When it was his turn, my lawyer first asked if he might approach the bench. The Judge allowed this, over Satan's strong objections, and beckoned him to come forward. As he got up and started walking I was able to see him now in his full splendor and majesty. Now I realized why he seemed so familiar, this was Jesus representing me—my Lord and my Savior.

He stopped at the bench and spoke softly to the Judge, then turned to address the court. "Satan was correct in saying that this man had sinned, I won't deny any of these allegations. And yes, the wages of sin is death, and this man deserves to be punished."

Jesus took a deep breath and turned to his Father with outstretched arms and proclaimed, "However, I died on the cross so that this person might have eternal life, and he has accepted me as his Savior, so he is mine."

My Lord continued with, "His name is written in the book of life, and no one can snatch him from me. Satan still does not understand yet, this man is not to be given justice but rather mercy."

As Jesus sat down, he quietly paused, looked at his Father and replied, "There is nothing else that needs to be done. I've done it all."

The Judge lifted his mighty hand and slammed the gavel down and the following words bellowed from his lips—"This man is free—the penalty for him has already been paid in full, case dismissed."

As my Lord led me away I could hear Satan ranting and raving, "I won't give up, I'll win the next one!"

I asked Jesus, as he gave me my instructions where to go next, "Have you ever lost a case?"

Christ lovingly smiled and said, "Everyone that has come to me and asked me to represent them has received the same verdict as you, 'Paid in full.'"

Music Lessons

KATHERINE BOND
FROM FOCUS ON THE FAMILY *CLUBHOUSE* MAGAZINE

obody asked if I wanted a "Junior High Buddy." I just got called to the office—where I practically lived anyway. Anything that went wrong at Orville Wright Elementary—the fifteen pairs of underwear up the flagpole, the urinal that played "Jingle Bells" whenever someone flushed—whatever it was, I got blamed.

Sitting in Mrs. Kellerman's office was a kid, older than me with skinny brown arms. He grinned real fast when I came in.

"Kyle, this is Austin Atterberry." Mrs. Kellerman stuck a fat file—mine—back in the cabinet. "Austin is an eighth grader at Edison. He's agreed to be your Junior High Buddy."

So when did I agree to it? I thought.

The kid stood up. He was tall, real tall.

"I bet you play basketball," I said.

"Nope," he said, "piano."

It's not like I needed looking after. My parents worked and the kids in my neighborhood already had friends, so I was used to being on my own. But every afternoon Austin was by my locker sucking on a sourball.

It wasn't bad, I guess. With Austin around no one beat me up.

He was right when he said he didn't play basketball. His throws always hit the rim. I beat him every time.

Austin shook his head when I showed how I'd wired our doorbell to open the neighbor's garage, but he had great ideas for my railroad.

The only thing that bugged Austin about my house was that there was no piano.

♫♪

"Here she is." Austin ran his hands over a Yamaha PR-500 keyboard. We were at Harmony Music.

"Mrs. Goodwin says if a piano won't fit in the apartment, this is the next best thing." Mrs. Goodwin taught Austin piano. He washed her windows for it, even though she said he didn't have to. If someone gave me a freebie, I wouldn't go pay for it.

"I've made six months of payments," he said. "Only a hundred dollars to go."

"How'd you get all that money?"

"Oh, mowing lawns, babysitting."

"Babysitting. What does my dad pay to keep me busy?"

Austin turned sharply. "No one pays me. I do this because I want to."

I didn't believe him. "Well, play something," I said.

When Austin hit "power," a scowling clerk bustled over. "Do you need help, boys?" he asked. "These are sensitive instruments—for *musicians.*"

"How do you know we're not *musicians?*" I imitated his snobby voice. "For your information, Austin practically *owns—*"

"Chill, Kyle," Austin cut in. "The man's new; the manager knows me." He nodded and stepped around the clerk, who immediately began polishing the keyboard where Austin's hands had been.

On the sidewalk, Austin stuck a sourball in his cheek.

"What a bigshot scumbag," I huffed. "Why'd you let him do that?"

"Here," said Austin. He handed me a sourball. I put it in my mouth and it felt like all the spit was being vacuumed off the back of my throat.

"If you're going to be a man, little bro', you gotta turn the other cheek," said Austin.

"Why?" I hucked the sourball onto the sidewalk. "So I can get punched twice?"

Austin put his hand on my shoulder. "Little bro', you need a good dose of Jesus."

I shook him off fast. "Jesus?!" I imagined myself in shiny shoes, polishing a Bible. "Not me. No way. No how."

"Uh-huh." Austin folded his arms. "It's the ones who fight it the most that want it the worst."

"Guess again," I said.

♫

Austin's church smelled of mildew and paint. I didn't want to be there, but Mrs. Goodwin had asked Austin to come early.

"Great echo!" I bounced my basketball. Austin gave me a look.

He sat at the piano while I doodled visitor cards. He played quietly at first, but the music grew. It whirlpooled around me. I felt like someone had opened a door in my chest and poured the notes in. "Wow!" I said when he was done. "What was that?"

"Just something I made up."

"Beautiful!" A lady stepped in, with bracelets up and down her arms. "Austin, you make an old woman cry."

"You must be Kyle." She smiled. "Take Austin downstairs, Kyle. There's something he should see."

Downstairs was a kitchen, some scratched tables and a couple high chairs. Then we saw it. Against the wall, was Austin's Yamaha PR-500!

"Mrs. Goodwin!" Austin let out his breath. "How did you...?"

Her bracelets jingled. "You've earned it, sugar," she said. "You've washed enough windows. Now it's my turn."

"You've already—"

"Hush, boy. Let an old woman have her way."

Austin turned on the keyboard. He made it sound like a violin, he played drum rhythms, he made it sound like an angel choir.

"Hey," I asked him, "can you make it sound like it's belching?"

"Try again," said Austin.

♪♪

When Austin went upstairs, I offered to babysit the keyboard. It was pretty cool. It could do trumpets and organ and something called "vibraphone."

Then, I got an idea. If I could make a urinal pay Jingle Bells, it would be easy to move a few wires and see if I could get a cow, a sheep and a chicken. Austin would bust a gut laughing.

I found a screwdriver and took off the back. I pulled the circuit board, messed with it and reinstalled it. Then I pressed a key. It sounded exactly like a strangled duck. I pressed another key. Same thing. No bells, no drums, just a shriek ending in a puttering wheeze.

Overhead the piano stopped. There were footsteps on the stairs. I shoved wires back into the keyboard as fast as I could.

Austin burst in and stopped. He looked at my fistful of wires. Without saying a word, he jammed a sourball in his mouth and left.

I found him on his knees in the sanctuary. Mrs. Goodwin was gone.

"What are you doing?" I asked.

"I'm praying I don't kill you," he muttered through the sourball.

It was a good time to go back downstairs. I messed with more wires. Nothing worked. It wasn't *my* fault it had so many circuits. If Austin was going to be that way, there was no reason to stay.

There was a sour taste in my mouth as I rode the bus home.

♪♪

Austin didn't show the next day. A week went by. It wasn't like I needed taking care of, but there was nothing to do. I couldn't even shoot hoops because I'd left my basketball at Austin's church.

I thought about all the basketball he'd played with me, even though he always lost. There were guys who sat with me at lunch and laughed when I made milk come out my nose, but Austin was a real friend.

And I wasn't.

I decided I really needed my basketball.

Austin was playing the church piano when I sneaked into the sanctuary. His sad music seeped inside me. Two stupid tears dripped down my nose.

When I went to wipe them, my basketball bounced to the floor.

Austin looked up. I looked down and blinked my eyes a bunch of times.

He walked up the aisle and put a hand on my shoulder. This time I didn't shake him off.

"I'm sorry," I mumbled, feeling the awfulness of what I'd done. "I tried to fix it, but—"

Austin nodded.

"Are you...still mad?" How lame. He probably hated me.

"Jesus says forgive," he said. "Forgive isn't a feeling, little bro'. It's something you do."

"Will you still be my Buddy?" I looked up at Austin and he grinned real fast.

"Yeah," he said. "I will, little bro'. There are a few things you've still gotta learn."

Be kind and compassionate to one another,
forgiving each other, just as in Christ God forgave you.

EPHESIANS 4:32

An Unspoken Promise

KRISTI POWERS

my father was not a sentimental man. I don't remember him ever oohing or ahhing over something I made as a child. Don't get me wrong. I knew that my dad loved me, but getting all mushy-eyed was not his thing. I learned that he showed me he loved me in other ways.

There was one particular moment when this became real to me…

I always believed that my parents had a good marriage, but just before I, the youngest of four children, turned sixteen, my belief was sorely tested. My father, who used to share in the chores around the house, gradually started becoming despondent. From the time he came home from his job at the factory, to the time he went to bed, he hardly spoke a word to my mom or us kids. The strain on Mom and Dad's relationship was very evident.

However, I was not prepared for the day that Mom sat my siblings and me down and told us that Dad had decided to leave. All that I could think of was that I was going to become a product of a divorced family. It was something I never thought possible, and it grieved me greatly. I kept telling myself that it wasn't going to happen, and I went totally numb when I knew my dad was really leaving. The night before he left I stayed up in my room for a long time. I prayed and I cried—and I wrote a long letter to my dad. I told him how much I loved him and how much I would miss him. I told him I was praying for him and wanted him to know that, no matter what, Jesus and I loved him. I told him that I would always and forever be his Krissie...his Noodles. As I folded my note, I stuck in a picture of me and a saying I had always heard. "Anyone can be a father but it takes someone special to be called a Daddy."

Early the next morning, as my Dad left our house, I snuck out to the car and slipped my letter into one of his bags.

Two weeks went by with hardly a word from my father. Then, one afternoon, I came home from school to find my mom sitting at the dining room table waiting to talk to me. I could see in her eyes that she had been crying. She told me that Dad had been there and they had had a very long talk. They decided that there were things that the both of them could and would change—and that their marriage was worth saving. Mom then turned her focus to my eyes—"Kristi, Dad told me that you wrote him a letter. Can I ask what you wrote to him?"

I found it hard to share with my mom what I wrote from my heart to Dad. I mumbled a few words and shrugged. Mom said, "Well, Dad said that when he read your letter, it made him cry. It meant a lot to him, and I have hardly ever seen your dad cry. After he read your letter, he called to ask if he could come over to talk. Whatever you said really made a difference to your dad."

A few days later, my dad was back. This time to stay. We never talked about the letter, my dad and I. I guess I always figured that it was something that was a secret between us.

My parents went on to be married a total of thirty-six years before my dad's early death, at the age of fifty-three, cut short their lives together. In the last sixteen years of my parent's marriage, all those who knew my mom and dad witnessed one of the truly "great" marriages. Their love grew stronger every day, and my heart swelled with pride as I saw them grow closer together.... When Mom and Dad received the news from the doctor that his heart was deteriorating rapidly, they took it hand in hand, side by side, all the way.

After Dad's death, we had the most unpleasant task of going through his things. I have never liked this task and opted to run errands so I did not have to be there while most of the things were divided and boxed up. When I got back from my errands, my brother said, "Kristi, Mom said to give this to you. She said you would know what it meant."

As I looked down into his outstretched hand I realized the impact of my letter so long ago. In my brother's hand was my picture that I had given my dad that day. My unsentimental dad, who never let his emotions get the best of him. My dad, who almost never outwardly showed his love for me, had kept the one thing that meant so much to him and me. I sat down and the tears began to flow—tears that I thought had dried up from the grief of his death now found new life as I realized what I meant to him.

Mom told me that Dad kept both the picture and that letter his whole life. I have a box in my home that I call the "Dad" box. In it are so many things that remind me of my dad. I pull that picture out every once in a while and remember. I remember a promise that was made many years ago between a young man and his bride on their wedding day. And I remember the unspoken promise that was made between a father and his daughter....

A promise kept.

virtue

Things of Beauty

*One of the most beautiful compensations
of this life is that no one can sincerely try
to help another without helping himself.*

RALPH WALDO EMERSON

The Day Lisa Lost

MICHAEL T. POWERS

I first met Lisa Kincaid on the volleyball court as she played for a rival high school in the conference I coach in. Many times I was on the opposing sidelines and could only watch in awe at her athleticism. The speed of a cheetah, the mental toughness of a veteran, and a thirty-two-inch vertical jump! (Unheard of for a high school girl. And she was only a sophomore!)

Starting her junior year, I was fortunate enough to coach Lisa on a USA Junior Olympic volleyball team, and it was during these two years that my wife and I grew to love and respect her. Respect, not only for her many athletic achievements, but for her unselfishness and humility to those around her in the face of the many honors that were bestowed upon her. Besides being one of the most coachable athletes I have ever had, she was the epitome of a team player and went out of her way to be humble.

If anyone had a right to be cocky or proud of herself, it was Lisa. Besides being one of the best volleyball and basketball players in the state, she became a track legend in the Dairy State. How good was she? She went sixty-four straight conference meets and never lost in any event she was entered in.

She made trips to the state finals all four years she was in high school and came away with six state titles. Many times she was the lone representative for her team at the state competition and would single-handedly place her high school as high as third. While she excelled in the triple jump, long jump, 100- and 200-meter dashes, there were times when her coach needed her to fill in for other events. One particular day he asked her to run the 300-meter hurdles. She had never competed in this event before, but the coach needed her that day for the good of the team. How did she do? She not only won, she set the school record in the first and only time she competed in that event!

Never once did she brag about her accomplishments. In fact, she felt uncomfortable talking about her achievements and would usually steer the conversation away from herself and to the performances of her younger sisters or other teammates.

Besides coaching her in volleyball, I was able to see her at many track meets, as I was hired to produce track videos by other high schools in the conference for my video production company. I saw many instances where she would loan her shoes to someone who forgot them or slow down at the end of a race to finish up stride for stride with her sister, both of them smiling from ear-to-ear as they crossed the finish line together. And I vividly remember Lisa going up to an athlete from a different team and wishing her a happy birthday. The young lady's face just beamed as she told Lisa of her birthday plans for later that night. I was smiling as I walked away, because I happened to know that it was Lisa's birthday that day too, but never once did she mention it to her.

But there was one particular track meet during Lisa's junior year where she impressed upon me what is still good about sports these days.

It was a nonconference meet late in the year, and Lisa's coach told her he needed her to run the mile. Lisa had never done so, but agreed to do what was best for the team. Lisa easily outdistanced the competition, but on the last lap, she "seemed" to grow tired. Two athletes from the other team passed her, and then so did Jane, Lisa's teammate. She was able to stay just behind her teammate and cross the finish line at her heels. Lisa "lost" an event for the first time in her track career.

You see, athletes in Lisa's track program need to earn a set amount of points in order to earn a varsity letter. Lisa knew that Jane, who was a senior, needed to finish at least third to earn a letter for the first time. Lisa also knew that the two athletes on the other team were most likely going to beat Jane, if they ran anywhere near the times they had been running all year, but that barring an injury during the race, Jane was a lock to finish third. But that was until the coach entered Lisa in the event.

Lisa remembered all of this as she lined up for the start of that race, and I had often wondered why she had a slight smile on her face after having lost for the first time ever.

After four years of working hard, Jane finally received her first varsity letter and helped her team win the meet.

And Lisa? On that day, she earned my respect and admiration, and in my mind, she solidified herself as the role model this generation sorely needs. The day Lisa lost.

Pursue a righteous life—
a life of wonder, faith, love, steadiness, courtesy.
Run hard and fast in the faith.

1 TIMOTHY 6:11–12
THE MESSAGE

The Final I Failed

BERNICE BROOKS
FROM *STUFF YOU DON'T HAVE TO PRAY ABOUT*

finals week had arrived with all its stress. I had been up late cramming for an exam. Now, as I slumped in my seat, I felt like a spring that had been wound too tight. I had two tests back-to-back, and I was anxious to get through with them. At the same time I expected to be able to maintain my straight-A grade-point average.

As I waited impatiently for the professor to arrive, a stranger walked up to the blackboard and began to write:

Due to a conflict, your professor is unable to give you your test in this classroom. He is waiting for you in the gymnasium.

Oh, great, I thought. *Now I have to walk clear across campus just to take this stupid exam.*

The entire class was scurrying out the door and rushing to the gym. No one wanted to be late for the final, and we weren't wasting time talking.

The route to the gym took us past the hospital. There was a man stumbling around in front of it. I recognized him as the young blind man whose wife had just given birth to a baby in that hospital. He had been there before, but he must have become confused.

Oh, well, I told myself. *Someone will come along soon and help him. I just don't have time to stop now.*

So I hurried along with the rest of the class on our way to take that final exam.

As we continued down the sidewalk, a woman came rushing out of a nearby bookstore. She had a baby on one arm, a stack of books on the other, and a worried look on her face. The books fell onto the sidewalk, and the baby began to cry as she stooped to pick them up.

She should have left that kid at home, I thought. I dodged her as the class and I rushed along.

Just around the next corner someone had left a dog on a leash tied to a tree. He was a big, friendly mutt, and we had all seen him there before, but today he couldn't quite reach the pan of water left for him. He was straining at his leash and whining.

I thought, *What cruel pet owner would tie up a dog and not leave his water where he could reach it?* But I hurried on.

As we neared the gym, a car passed us and parked close to the door. I recognized the man who got out as one of the maintenance crew. I also noticed he left the lights on.

"He's going to have a problem when he tries to start that car to go home tonight," the fellow next to me said.

By that time we were going in the doors of the gym. The maintenance man waved a greeting to us and disappeared down one of the halls. We found seats close to where our teacher waited.

The professor stood with his arms folded, looking at us. We looked back. The silence became uncomfortable. We all knew his tests were also teaching tools, and we wondered what he was up to. He motioned toward the door, and in walked the blind man, the young mother with her baby, a girl holding the big dog on a leash, and the maintenance man.

These people had been planted along the way in an effort to test whether or not the class had grasped the meaning behind the story of the Good Samaritan and the man who fell among thieves. We all failed.

"Now which of these three would you say was a neighbor to the man who was attacked by bandits?" Jesus asked. The man replied, "The one who showed him mercy."

LUKE 10:36–37
NEW LIVING TRANSLATION

Choosing Mary

DAN TAYLOR
FROM *LETTERS TO MY CHILDREN*

When I was in the sixth grade I was an all-American. I was smart, athletic, witty, handsome, and incredibly nice. Things went downhill fast in junior high, but for this one year at least, I had everything.

Of course I also had Miss Owens for an assistant teacher. She helped Mr. Jenkins, our regular teacher. She knew that even though I was smart and incredibly nice, there was still a thing or two I could work on.

One of the things you were expected to do in grade school was learn to dance. My parents may have had some reservations at first, but since this was square dancing, it was okay.

Every time we went to work on our dancing, we did this terrible thing. The boys would all line up at the door to our classroom. Then, one at a time, each boy would pick a girl to be his partner. The girls all sat at their desks. As they were chosen, they left their desks and joined the snot-nosed kids who had honored them with their favor.

Believe me, the boys did not like doing this—at least I didn't. But think about being one of those girls. Think about waiting to get picked. Think about seeing who was going to get picked before you. Think about worrying that you'd get picked by someone you couldn't stand. Think about worrying whether you were going to get picked at all!

Think if you were Mary. Mary sat near the front of the classroom on the right side. She wasn't pretty. She wasn't real smart. She wasn't witty. She was nice, but that wasn't enough in those days. And Mary certainly wasn't athletic. In fact, she'd had polio or something when she was younger; one of her arms was drawn up, and she had a bad leg, and to finish it off, she was kind of heavy.

Here's where Miss Owens comes in. Miss Owens took me aside one day and said, "Dan, next time we have square dancing, I want you to choose Mary."

Well she may as well have told me to fly to Mars. It was an idea that was so new and inconceivable that I could barely hold it in my head. You mean pick someone other than the best, the most pretty, the most popular, when my turn came? That seemed like breaking a law of nature or something.

And then Miss Owens did a rotten thing. She told me it was what a Christian should do. I knew immediately that I was doomed. I was doomed because I knew she was right. It was exactly the thing Jesus would have done. I was surprised, in fact, that I hadn't seen it on a Sunday school flannel board yet: "Jesus choosing the lame girl for the Yeshiva dance." It was bound to be somewhere in the Bible.

I agonized. Choosing Mary would go against all the coolness I had accumulated.

The day came when we were to square dance again. If God really loved me, I thought, He will make me last. Then picking Mary will cause no stir. I will have done the right thing, and it won't have cost me anything.

You can guess where I was instead. For whatever reason, Mr. Jenkins made me first in line. There I was, my heart pounding—now I knew how some of the girls must have felt.

The faces of the girls were turned towards me, some smiling. I looked at Mary and saw that she was half turned to the back of the room, her face staring down at her desk. Mr. Jenkins said, "Okay, Dan—choose your partner."

I remember feeling very far away. I heard my voice say, "I choose Mary."

Never has reluctant virtue been so rewarded. I still see her face undimmed in my memory. She lifted her head, and on her face, reddened with pleasure and surprise and embarrassment all at the same time, was the most genuine look of delight and even pride that I had ever seen, before or since. It was so pure that I had to look away because I knew I didn't deserve it.

Mary came and took my arm, as we had been instructed, and she walked beside me, bad leg and all, just like a princess.

Mary is my age now. I never saw her after that year. I don't know what her life's been like or what she's doing. But I'd like to think she has a fond memory of at least one day in sixth grade. I know I do.

Don't judge by his appearance or height....
The Lord doesn't make decisions the way you do!
People judge by outward appearance,
but the Lord looks at a person's thoughts and intentions.

1 Samuel 16:7
New Living Translation

Toothless Grin

SHARON PALMER

I was doing some last-minute Christmas shopping in a toy store and decided to look at fashion dolls. A nicely dressed little girl was excitedly looking through the same dolls as well, with a roll of money clamped tightly in her little hand. When she came upon a doll she liked, she would turn and ask her father if she had enough money to buy it. He usually said "yes," but she would keep looking and keep going through their ritual of "do I have enough?"

As she was looking, a little boy wandered in across the aisle and started sorting through some of the video games. He was dressed neatly, but in clothes that were obviously rather worn, and wearing a jacket that was probably a couple of sizes too small. He, too, had money in his hand, but it looked to be no more than five dollars or so, at the most. He was with his father as well, but each time he picked one of the video games and looked at his father, his father shook his head.

The little girl had apparently chosen her doll, a beautifully dressed, glamorous creation that would have been the envy of every little girl on the block. However, she had stopped and was watching the interchange between the little boy and his father. Rather dejectedly, the boy had given up on the video games and had chosen what looked like a book of stickers instead. He and his father then started walking through another aisle of the store.

The little girl put her carefully chosen doll back on the shelf and ran over to the video games. She excitedly picked up one that was lying on top of the other toys, and raced toward the checkout after speaking with her father. I picked up my purchases and got in line behind them. Then, much to the little girl's obvious delight, the little boy and his father got in line behind me.

After the toy was paid for and bagged, the little girl handed it back to the cashier and whispered something in her ear. The cashier smiled and put the package under the counter. I paid for my purchases and was rearranging things in my purse when the little boy came up to the cashier.

The cashier rang up his purchases and then said, "Congratulations, you have been selected to win a prize!" With that, she handed the little boy the video game, and he could only stare in disbelief. It was, he said, exactly what he had wanted!

The little girl and her father had been standing at the doorway during all of this, and I saw the biggest, prettiest, toothless grin on that little girl that I have ever seen in my life. Then they walked out the door, and I followed, close behind them.

As I walked back to my car, in amazement over what I had just witnessed, I heard the father ask his daughter why she had done that. I'll never forget what she said to him. "Daddy, didn't Nana and PawPaw want me to buy something that would make me happy?" He said, "Of course they did, honey." To which the little girl replied, "Well, I just did!" With that, she giggled and started skipping toward their car.

I had just witnessed the Christmas spirit in that toy store, in the form of a little girl who understands more about the reason for the season than most adults I know! May God bless her and her parents, just as she blessed that little boy, and me, that day!

It Really Didn't Matter

CHARLES COLSON
FROM *THE BODY*

The young people at Shively Christian Church, led at the time by Youth Pastor Dave Stone, were fiercely competitive with their neighbor, Shively Baptist, in all things, especially softball. They were also serious about their Christianity, faithfully attending the summer Bible camp led by the youth pastor.

One week the Bible lesson was about Jesus washing His disciples' feet, from John 13. To make the servanthood lesson stick, Pastor Stone divided the kids into groups and told them to go out and find a practical way to be servants.

"I want you to be Jesus in the city for the next two hours," he said. "If Jesus were here, what would He do? Figure out how He would help people."

Two hours later the kids reconvened in Pastor Stone's living room to report what they had done.

One group had done two hours of yard work for an elderly man. Another group bought ice cream treats and delivered them to several widows in the church. A third group visited a church member in the hospital and gave him a card. Another group went to a nursing home and sang Christmas carols—yes, Christmas carols in the middle of August. One elderly resident remarked that it was the warmest Christmas she could remember.

But when the fifth group stood up and reported what they had done, everyone groaned. This group had made its way to none other than their arch rival, Shively Baptist, where they had asked the pastor if he knew someone who needed help. The pastor sent them to the home of an elderly woman who needed yard work done. There, for two hours, they mowed grass, raked the yard, and trimmed hedges.

When they were getting ready to leave, the woman called the group together and thanked them for their hard work. "I don't know how I could get along without you," she told them. "You kids at Shively Baptist are always coming to my rescue."

"Shively Baptist!" interrupted Pastor Stone. "I sure hope you set her straight and told her you were from Shively *Christian* Church."

"Why, no, we didn't," the kids said. "We didn't think it mattered."

You will find, as you look back upon your life
that the moments that stand out are the moments
when you have done things for others.

HENRY DRUMMOND

A Brother Like That

DAN CLARK

A friend of mine named Paul received an automobile from his brother as a present. On Christmas Eve when Paul came out of his office, a street urchin was walking around the shiny new car, admiring it. "Is this your car, Mister?" he asked.

Paul nodded. "My brother gave it to me for Christmas." The boy was astounded. "You mean your brother gave it to you and it didn't cost you nothing? Boy, I wish…" He hesitated.

Of course Paul knew what he was going to wish for. He was going to wish he had a brother like that. But what the lad said jarred Paul all the way down to his heels.

"I wish," the boy went on, "that I could be a brother like that."

Paul looked at the boy in astonishment, then impulsively he added, "Would you like to take a ride in my automobile?"

"Oh yes, I'd love that."

After a short ride, the boy turned and with his eyes aglow, said, "Mister, would you mind driving in front of my house?"

Paul smiled a little. He thought he knew what the lad wanted. He wanted to show his neighbors that he could ride home in a big automobile. But Paul was wrong again.

"Will you stop where those two steps are?" the boy asked.

He ran up the steps. Then in a little while Paul heard him coming back, but he was not coming fast. He was carrying his little crippled brother. He sat him down on the bottom step, then sort of squeezed up against him and pointed to the car.

"There she is, Buddy, just like I told you upstairs. His brother gave it to him for Christmas and it didn't cost him a cent. And some day I'm gonna give you one just like it…then you can see for yourself all the pretty things in the Christmas windows that I've been trying to tell you about."

Paul got out and lifted the lad to the front seat of his car. The older brother climbed in beside him, and the three of them began a memorable holiday ride.

That Christmas Eve, Paul learned what Jesus meant when he had said, "It is more blessed to give…"

You can give without loving,
but you cannot love without giving.

AMY CARMICHAEL

The Drive-Through

MICHELLE METJE

dear Editor,
I think I might be the one that your staff is looking for. I don't know, though, if what I did the other day was anything to commend.... Actually, let me just tell you my side of the story, and maybe you will understand.

That day (last Monday) had been a really bad one. My sister was in the hospital fighting breast cancer, my brother's infant son had just been diagnosed with Cerebral Palsy, my husband and I had been arguing, and the kids wanted gifts that we couldn't afford to give them. The dog had tracked mud into the house (which was already a complete and utter mess), the baby was screaming, my back ached, and I had a sinus infection.... And none of it seemed to be getting any better. So I did what any normal person would do, I went to the Taco Hut. I knew I couldn't afford it, but I deserved a break.

So, as I sat there in the line at the drive-through counting the change in my coin purse and trying to figure out what I could afford, I said a prayer. "Lord, I know You are out there, but sometimes it is hard to believe that You care about what is going on in the world. If You did, why would all of this be happening at once? None of this is within my control, and no one can help me, but You can...and I feel like You won't.... It would all make it worthwhile if I could just know that You hear my prayers.... I know it is asking a lot, but can You, please, just give me some sort of sign that You are hearing me? Some sign that there is still Your kindness in the world. You don't even have to make all of my problems disappear, just let me know You hear my prayers."

My prayer was interrupted by the voice on the speaker. I ordered and pulled through to pay. I was pleased that I had enough money to pay for what I had ordered and an extra dollar leftover…like I said, money is kind of tight. I had already forgotten my prayer.

Now, patient sir, you must be wondering what this all has to do with what happened later…this is where it actually began.

As I paid the boy at the window, I heard a small voice say, "Give him your extra dollar." Just as plain as that. No crashing thunder, no orchestra in the background—just "Give him your dollar." I don't know why I followed the voice, I just did. I looked at the boy and said, "This is going to seem strange to you, but I want you to take this and apply it to their bill." I pointed to the car behind me, "Then I want you to tell them Merry Christmas."

The boy's face shined with excitement as he said, "Cool!"

That was all I knew. I went on with my day and didn't give it a second thought. I don't know why. I suppose you might think it odd to just give away money like that…just because a voice told you to do it. But for some strange reason, it just seemed right to me.

And like I said, I continued with my day—no more thought of the prayer, or the dollar…until Thursday morning.

I walked my children to the end of my driveway—like I do every school day—and picked up my husband's newspaper. Though I seldom read the silly thing (no offense), I always bring it in so it doesn't get wet or torn up before my husband can read it. I waved good-bye to the boys as they boarded the school bus and went inside with your publication under my arm. The baby hadn't awakened yet, and there was nothing worth watching on television, so I decided to open the paper and see if there was a good sale flyer that day.

And lo and behold, there was the headline: TACO HUT HERO SOUGHT. (A bit cheesy, wasn't it?) It caught my eye because I had just eaten there a couple of days before. And there, within the pages, the story was told about how a small act of kindness helped a family of six through a desperate time.

Kind sir, how was I to know that the woman behind me wouldn't accept my gift? That she would instead double it for the couple following her in line? I had no idea that each customer that ate at the Taco Hut that day would be offered the same money, and that each would refuse the gift only to increase it! One dollar (I have read) turned into more than $2500 by the end of business that day! By your paper's account, people were coming by just to offer their money to add to the fund! The whole time never knowing why they were giving, just doing it in the spirit of Christmas. All while I was at home scrubbing my bathroom floors!

Imagine my surprise to learn about the family that walked in the door at five minutes till closing.... Their car had broken down five miles down the highway.... Was it too late to order six tacos and six waters? Since reading your article, I have often thought about the four children with their dirty faces eating what must have seemed an extravagant dinner for the six travelers, homeless as they were, without hope for the coming Holiday.

Your paper had a picture of the same teen smiling from ear-to-ear.... His manager had given the travelers the money they had raised that day. It was enough to pay for a real meal, the repairs to their car, a night's stay at the Sleep Inn, their first month's rent, (I understand that they will be staying in this area now), and a few presents for under their tree. The boy had been asked how that made him feel, and he had answered, "Cool."

But, contrary to what you have reported in your article, dear Editor, that does not make me a hero...that makes for an answered prayer. How could this have been an answer to my prayer? Easily. I had asked for a sign that God still cared. I had asked for a sign that His kindness was still alive in the world. I had asked for a sign that He heard my prayers, and He answered me. Through the acts of my fellow man, through the faith of a community, through a young man with a one-word vocabulary...He answered me. And to quote a very sweet young man, in all of his wisdom, that's just plain "cool."

If God hadn't been working that day, none of this would have happened.

So, dear friend, if you are looking for the Hero of Taco Hut, look toward heaven. I don't think He is giving interviews anymore, but I am sure that if you have any questions, He will answer them.

I know that He answered mine. I know that all of my problems are small in comparison to His Greatness, and that He can handle anything. Please remind your readers of this. In the meantime, I will withhold my name.

May God Bless you, and Merry Christmas,

The Tool of the Taco Hut Hero

We must not only give what we have;
we must also give what we are.

CARDINAL MERCIA

Only One

EDWARD EVERETT HALE

I am only one,
But still I am one.
I cannot do everything,
But still I can do something;
And because I cannot do everything,
I will not refuse to do the something that I can do.

Jake's Gift

AUTHOR UNKNOWN

bill was a big, awkward, homely guy. He dressed oddly, with ill-fitting clothes.

There were several fellows who thought it smart to make fun of him. One day, one fellow noticed a small tear in his shirt and gave it a small rip. Another worker in the factory added his bit, and before long there was quite a ribbon dangling.

Bill went on about his work, and as he passed too near a moving belt the shirt strip was sucked into the machinery. In a split second, the sleeve and Bill were in trouble.

Alarms were sounded, switches were pulled, and trouble was avoided. The foreman, however, aware of what had happened, summoned the men and related this story:

In my younger days I worked in a small factory. That's when I first met Mike. He was big and witty, was always making jokes and playing little pranks. Mike was a leader. Then there was Pete who was a follower. He always went along with Mike. And then there was a man named Jake.

He was a little older than the rest of us—quiet, harmless, apart. He always ate his lunch by himself. He wore the same patched trousers for three years straight. He never entered into the games we played at noon, wrestling, horseshoes, and such. He appeared to be indifferent, always sitting quietly alone under a tree instead. Jake was a natural target for practical jokes. He might find a live frog in his dinner pail or a dead rodent in his hat.

But he always took it in good humor. Then one fall, when things were slack, Mike took off a few days to go hunting. Pete went along, of course. And they promised all of us that if they got anything they'd bring us each a piece.

So we were all quite excited when we heard that they'd returned and that Mike had gotten a really big buck. We heard more than that. Pete could never keep anything to himself, and it leaked out that they had a real whopper to play on Jake. Mike had cut up the critter and had made a nice package for each of us, and for the laugh, for the joke of it, he had saved the ears, the tail, and the hoofs. It would be so funny when Jake unwrapped them. Mike distributed his packages during the noon hour. We each got a nice piece, opened it, and thanked him. The biggest package of all he saved until last. It was for Jake.

Pete was all but bursting, and Mike looked very smug.

Like always, Jake sat by himself; he was on the far side of the big table. Mike pushed the package over to where he could reach it, and we all sat and waited. Jake was never one to say much. You might never know that he was around for all the talking he did. In three years he'd never said a hundred words. So we were all quite astounded with what happened next.

He took the package firmly in his grip and rose slowly to his feet. He smiled broadly at Mike—and it was then we noticed that his eyes were glistening. His Adam's apple bobbed up and down for a moment, and then he got control of himself.

"I knew you wouldn't forget me," he said gratefully. "I knew you'd come through! You're big and you're playful, but I knew all along that you had a good heart." He swallowed again and then took in the rest of us. "I know I haven't seemed too chummy with you men, but I never meant to be rude. You see, I've got nine kids at home—and a wife that's been an invalid—bedfast for four years now. She ain't ever going to get any better. And sometimes when she's real bad off, I have to sit up all night to take care of her. And most of my wages have had to go for doctors and medicine. The kids do all they can to help out, but at times it's been hard to keep food in their mouths. Maybe you think it's funny that I go off by myself to eat my dinner. Well, I guess I've been a little ashamed, because I don't always have anything between my sandwich. Or like today—maybe there's only a raw turnip in my pail. But I want you to know that this meat really means a lot to me. Maybe more than to anybody here because tonight my kids…" he wiped the tears from his eyes with the back of his hand, "…tonight my kids will have a really…"

He tugged at the string. We'd been watching Jake so intently we hadn't paid much notice to Mike and Pete. But we all noticed them now, because they both dove at once to grab the package. But they were too late. Jake had broken the wrapper and was already surveying his present. He examined each hoof, each ear, and then he held up the tail. It wiggled limply. It should have been so funny, but nobody laughed—nobody at all. But the hardest part was when Jake looked up and said, "Thank you," while trying to smile.

Silently each man moved forward carrying his package and quietly placed it in front of Jake for they had suddenly realized how little their own gift had really meant to them…until now.

This was where the foreman left the story and the men.

He didn't need to say any more; but it was gratifying to notice that as each man ate his lunch that day, they shared part with Bill and one fellow even took off his shirt and gave it to him.

All of you should be of one mind,
full of sympathy toward each other,
loving one another with tender hearts and humble minds.

1 PETER 3:8
NEW LIVING TRANSLATION

Rescue at Sea

DAN CLARK

Years ago, in a small fishing village in Holland, a young boy taught the world about the rewards of unselfish service. Because the entire village revolved around the fishing industry, a volunteer rescue team was needed in cases of emergency. One night the winds raged, the clouds burst, and a gale force storm capsized a fishing boat at sea. Stranded and in trouble, the crew sent out the SOS. The captain of the rescue rowboat team sounded the alarm, and the villagers assembled in the town square overlooking the bay. While the team launched their rowboat and fought their way through the wild waves, the villagers waited restlessly on the beach, holding lanterns to light the way back.

An hour later, a rescue boat reappeared through the fog, and the cheering villagers ran to greet them. Falling exhausted on the sand, the volunteers reported that the rescue boats could not hold any more passengers, and they had to leave one man behind. Even one more passenger would have surely capsized the rescue boat, and all would have been lost.

Frantically, the captain called for another volunteer team to go after the lone survivor. Sixteen-year-old Hans stepped forward. His mother grabbed his arm, pleading, "Please don't go. Your father died in a shipwreck ten years ago, and your older brother, Paul, has been lost at sea for three weeks. Hans, you are all I have left."

Hans replied, "Mother, I have to go. What if everyone said, 'I can't go, let someone else do it?' Mother, this time I have to do my duty. When the call for service comes, we all need to take our turn and do our part." Hans kissed his mother, joined the team, and disappeared into the night.

Another hour passed, which seemed to Hans's mother like an eternity. Finally, the rescue boat darted through the fog with Hans standing up in the bow. Cupping his hands the captain called, "Did you find the lost man?" Barely able to contain himself, Hans excitedly yelled back, "Yes, we found him. Tell my mother it's my older brother, Paul!"

A friend is always loyal, and a brother
is born to help in time of need.

PROVERBS 17:17
NEW LIVING TRANSLATION

A Father with an Educated Heart

LaVonn Steiner

We come by business naturally in our family. Each of the seven children in our family worked in our father's store, "Our Own Hardware-Furniture Store," in Mott, North Dakota, a small town on the prairie. We started working by doing odd jobs like dusting, arranging shelves, and wrapping, and later graduated to serving customers. As we worked and watched, we learned that work was about more than survival and making a sale. One lesson stands out in my mind.

It was shortly before Christmas. I was in the eighth grade and was working evenings, straightening the toy section. A little boy, five or six years old, came in. He was wearing a brown, tattered coat with dirty, worn cuffs. His hair was straggly, except for a cowlick that stood straight up from the crown of his head. His shoes were scuffed, and his one shoelace was torn.

The little boy looked poor to me—too poor to afford to buy anything. He looked around the toy section, picked up this item and that, and carefully put them back in their place.

Dad came down the stairs and walked over to the boy. His steel blue eyes smiled and the dimple in his cheek stood out as he asked the boy what he could do for him.

The boy said he was looking for a Christmas present to buy his brother.

I was impressed that Dad treated him with the same respect as any adult. Dad told him to take his time and look around.

He did.

After about twenty minutes, the little boy carefully picked up a toy plane, walked up to my dad and said, "How much for this, Mister?"

"How much you got?" Dad asked.

The little boy held out his hand and opened it. His hand was creased with wet lines of dirt from clutching his money. In his hand lay two dimes, a nickel, and two pennies—27 cents. The price on the toy plane he'd picked out was $3.98.

"That'll just about do it," Dad said as he closed the sale. Dad's reply still rings in my ears.

I thought about what I'd seen as I wrapped the present. When the little boy walked out of the store, I didn't notice the dirty, worn coat, the straggly hair, or the single torn shoelace.

What I saw was a radiant child with a treasure. I also saw my father's educated heart.

Change of Heart

LINDA THERESA RACZEK

ory Willis sat in his dad's truck, wondering what he'd gotten himself into. Mrs. Bartelucci had a mean reputation. She was old and cranky and complained about everything and everyone—not exactly the kind of person a sixteen-year-old would hang out with.

But his youth pastor's words were still ringing in his ears: "It's time to put feet on your faith. It's time to reach out. The forgotten. The lonely. The misunderstood. Do you love God enough to love them?"

Mrs. B. was on the church's list of shut-ins. Cory had volunteered to bring her groceries and to spend a few Saturday afternoons doing chores, running errands—whatever she needed.

As Cory lugged the box of groceries to the door, he could see an elderly lady staring at him through the kitchen window.

"Mrs. Bar… uh, Mrs. B.!" he yelled. "I'm from the church!"

She swung open the door, her face angry. "I'm old, not deaf!" she snapped.

"Now don't just stand there like a statue; bring in my food." Cory set the box on the kitchen table. Mrs. B. peered in and turned up her nose. "This isn't fit to eat," she said.

The room was too warm and smelled of mothballs. Cory watched as Mrs. B. put on a threadbare sweater. She was a tiny question-mark-shaped woman. He had never seen anyone so bent over. Unless she craned her neck to look right at him, he was always looking at the wispy white hair on the top of her head.

Mrs. B. reached out and handed him a rake, work gloves, and some black plastic bags.

Cory followed her out into the yard.

"Stand here," she said. Cory hesitated, then started raking.

"I said stand!" she said, annoyed. "You just watch." She snatched back the rake. Mrs. B. was very particular—first raking loosely into a large pile, then scooping up leaves with a rusty dustpan and pouring them carefully into a plastic bag. Finally, she raked all over again in the same spot.

After a while she showed him how to hold the bag open for her, his hands held just so. She continued with her raking, slowly and methodically. *At this rate,* Cory thought, *we'll be raking leaves through Christmas vacation.*

"Mrs. B., why don't you go lie down?" he said hopefully. "I'll finish, okay?" She narrowed her eyes at him. "Lie down, indeed! I'm old, not *dead*," she said sharply. "At least not yet."

A little while later, she added, "Well, my back does hurt. We'll just put these things up, and you can come back tomorrow."

"But..."

"Tomorrow."

It was the start of a bad pattern. She couldn't do more than a small section of lawn at a time, but she wouldn't let him help, except to hold the bag. She was just so bossy, so picky. He didn't feel free to say no to the next day—or the next.

One day, as Mrs. B. was bending over to scoop up some leaves, Cory saw that she was in pain. It was amazing to think she did this alone every year. "Mrs. B.," he said, "I need to learn how to do this stuff. Why don't we at least take turns scooping up the leaves. You can tell me if I'm doing it wrong." She gave him a suspicious look. "You bet I will!" she growled.

They took turns. She criticized. At first he felt irritated with her, but then he made a game of it. He tried to see if he could do it exactly as she wanted. She never dished out compliments, so he settled for silence. If she didn't say anything, he gave himself a point. He took away points for mean looks, sassy comments, and outright insults.

That meant he was always in the hole!

Mrs. B. was crankier when she stumbled, then struggled to catch herself. Cory soon realized that she was a proud person, and that being so old and bent over was embarrassing for her.

Cory liked it best when she held open the bag and he scooped, especially if people were going by. He liked the way they looked at him helping Mrs. B. One day Cory thought to bring his own rake, and they took turns at that, too. "My dad doesn't even rake this good, Mrs. B.," he commented, dragging another plump bag of leaves over to the alley.

"Well, you have to keep things up," she said briskly. But then she added, as if to herself, "Somebody could get the idea you belong in a nursing home." Cory mulled over that comment. The thought of having his freedom taken away—being sent away from his parents against his will—scared him. In some small way, he felt as if he was finally beginning to understand Mrs. B.

One Saturday she was pale when she came to the door.

She pushed her uncombed hair out of her eyes. "You have to go. I don't feel up to working."

Part of him leaped at the thought of having his Saturday free, but he said, "That's okay, Mrs. B. We'll just take turns like always. I'll do mine now and you take your turn tomorrow."

Cory expected her to refuse outright, but she wavered. "Okay, I guess." Encouraged, Cory began, "You just go rest and…"

But sparks flew from Mrs. B.'s bleary eyes. "Are you patronizing me?" she croaked.

"I don't even know what that means!" Cory said defensively.

"It means don't talk down to me as if I'm a child," she said. "I'm old, not stupid!"

Cory stomped off, angry and hurt. A storm was supposed to be coming in a few days, and the remaining leaves could either blow all over the clean part of the yard or get packed under the first snow. Did he care?

On Monday, however, no one answered the door. Cory peeked through the window and was surprised Mrs. B.'s dishes weren't done. He banged harder and could imagine her muttering, "I'm old, not deaf!" But Mrs. B. didn't come to the door.

She must still be mad, he thought bitterly. *Well, so am I.* Cory decided to wash his hands of the whole affair. She was on her own. It would be good to have his life back.

That evening, the phone rang, and his mom glanced over at him with concern. "What?" he said. "Am I in trouble?"

"Honey, Pastor Wheeler thought you'd want to know that Mrs. B.'s in the hospital. He said you were the only kid she's ever let help her. Maybe she's better off in a nursing home."

Cory felt guilty. He pushed his chair back and stood up. "Don't even think it, Mom," he said. "Dad, can I borrow the truck? I have something important to do."

Cory felt nervous as he walked down the bright hall of the hospital, his shoes squeaking on the shiny linoleum. At the nurse's station he asked for Mrs. Bartelucci's room.

The nurse stared at him over half-moon lenses. "Sorry, young man. It's past visiting hours."

He felt his chest tighten. "Could I write her a note?" he asked hopefully. "Mrs. B. is a friend of mine."

The nurse didn't answer, but handed him a small square of note paper. Cory printed out a simple message:

MRS. B.—FRONT YARD IS A MESS. COME HOME SOON. WE'VE GOT WORK TO DO!—CORY

He watched the nurse take it into Mrs. B.'s room. His elderly friend raised her head weakly and looked at him. He gave her a little wave. When she nodded, she had a faint grin on her face.

It was the first time he'd ever seen her smile.

Cory smiled back. Then his youth pastor's words flooded his thoughts again: "The forgotten. The lonely. The misunderstood."

Cory felt as if he was finally beginning to understand Mrs. B.—and what it means to put feet on one's faith.

When Winning Took a Backseat

BRUCE NASH AND ALLAN ZULLO
FROM *THE GREATEST SPORTS STORIES NEVER TOLD*

Scott Bennett and Brad Howes grew up south of Salt Lake City in the fertile valley between the Jordan River and the towering Wasatch Mountains of Utah. The boys lived just far enough apart not to attend the same schools, but close enough to compete in the same leagues in baseball, football, and basketball.

No matter whose team won, Scott and Brad always shook hands and complimented each other on the way they played. The two didn't become close friends because they were always on opposite sides. But the boys grew up admiring each other's skills.

It happened while the boys were members of school cross-country teams—Scott at Murray High and Brad at nearby Cottonwood High. During meets, as they pounded out mile after mile across the empty fields, Scott and Brad formed an unspoken bond. They learned to respect one another's competitive spirit and strengths. Brad liked to set a blistering pace early in the race, which wore down most other runners who tried to keep up with him. Scott, meanwhile, had a strong finishing kick, which had him breathing down the leader's neck on the final stretch.

Usually, the boys finished first and second when their schools competed. Sometimes Brad won; other times it was Scott who broke the tape first.

Their most memorable race—the one track and field coaches still talk about—occurred during a cross-country regional meet, with the winner going to the state finals. The event, held as part of Cottonwood High's homecoming festivities, was run during halftime of the football game between Cottonwood and Murray. Since the schools were only about ten miles apart, the stands were jammed with rooters from both sides.

At halftime, Murray was leading by two touchdowns and threatening to spoil Cottonwood's homecoming. So when Scott and Brad took their places at the starting line, each knew there was a lot more at stake than just a race. Brad felt that by winning he could salvage some of Cottonwood's pride at homecoming. Scott wanted to win to prove that Murray was the best at everything.

There were three other runners in the race, but all eyes were on Scott and Brad when the starter's gun went off. The group circled the track that ringed the football field and headed out the exit for the 2.6-mile cross-country run.

As expected, Brad quickly took the lead in a race that went through the rolling, grassy hills of Sugarhouse Park bordering the school grounds. At the halfway point, Brad had pulled ahead of Scott by nearly 300 yards while the other runners had fallen out of contention.

Despite the gap, Scott wasn't worried. In past races, Brad usually grabbed the lead, but Scott, with his strong finish, often caught Brad on the final stretch. Sticking to his race strategy, Scott steadily gained on Brad. By the time the two reached the stadium, Scott was only a couple of steps behind.

When the pair dashed through the stadium tunnel and onto the track for the final lap, the capacity crowd rose to its feet to cheer the runners who were now racing stride for stride.

But coming around the final turn, Scott cut to the inside to pass Brad and get in position for a sprint down the stretch. Just then, Brad also moved inside and the runners' legs tangled. Both stumbled. Scott managed to keep his feet, but Brad sprawled headfirst onto the track.

Scott ran a few more paces. But suddenly, he became aware of an eerie silence. The crowd that had been shouting moments before fell deathly silent when Brad tripped and hit the ground. So Scott stopped and looked back at his lifelong rival. Brad, whose knees and hands were scraped and bleeding from falling on the cinders, was struggling to regain his feet. Who won or lost the race no longer mattered to Scott. His friend and competitor was hurt. Scott knew what he had to do—he went back to help. "Give me your hand, Brad," said Scott. "Let me help you."

Brad looked up at Scott, smiled, and said, "Man, you're something else." Scott pulled his injured rival to his feet but Brad was hurting so badly that he couldn't run very well. So Scott put his arm around Brad and the two began trotting down the final stretch. The thousands of fans in the stands gasped when they saw Scott's gallant gesture and then erupted into thunderous applause.

Shocked by the unexpected spill, the track judges had dropped the tape that marked the finish line. "Get that tape back up!" a coach yelled. "They're coming in—together!"

With Brad limping the final 50 yards, and Scott helping him every step of the way, the two competitors crossed the finish line arm in arm. The coaches and the track judges then huddled over what to do about the incredibly unselfish act of sportsmanship they had just witnessed.

"One of the runners has to win, but that doesn't mean the other one has to lose," said Scott's coach, Sam Moore. "I know Scott wouldn't want to have his victory tainted. I say we give both kids first place."

Moore's suggestion won unanimous approval from Brad's coach and the judges. The race was declared a dead heat.

"I have never seen such sportsmanship," said Moore. "I doubt if I ever will again."

Humility brings honor.

PROVERBS 29:23B
NEW LIVING TRANSLATION

sharing your faith

Everything

If you meet me and you forget about me
you have lost nothing of value.
If you meet Jesus Christ and forget about him
you have lost everything of value.

AUTHOR UNKNOWN

The Shadow of the Cross

AUTHOR UNKNOWN

While taking a class in photography at the University of Cincinnati, a Christian became acquainted with a young man named Charles Murray who also was a student at the school and training for the summer Olympics as a high diver.

Charles was very patient, listening to him for hours about how Jesus had saved him. Charles was not raised in a home that attended any kind of church, so all that was told to him was a fascination. He even began to ask questions about forgiveness of sin.

Finally, the day came that the question was put to him, "Have you realized your need of a Redeemer, and are you ready to trust Christ as your Savior?" His countenance fell and the guilt was in his face. But his reply was a strong "No."

In the days that followed, he was quiet and often avoided the believer until one day Charles decided to call him. He wanted to know where to look in the New Testament for some verses about salvation. He declined to meet but thanked the Christian for the Scripture references. He was greatly troubled but was not ready to receive help.

Because he was training for the Olympic games, Charles had special privileges at the University pool facilities. Some time between 10:30 and 11:00 that evening, he decided to go swim and practice a few dives. It was a clear night in October, and the moon was big and bright. The University pool was housed under a ceiling of glass panes, so the moon shone bright across the top of the wall in the pool area.

Charles climbed to the highest platform to take his first dive. At that moment the Spirit of God began to convict him of his sins. All the scripture he had read, all the occasions of witnessing to him about Christ flooded his mind.

He stood on the platform backwards to make his dive, spread his arms to gather his balance, looked up to the wall, and saw his own shadow caused by the light of the moon. It was in the shape of a cross. He could bear the burden of his sin no longer. His heart broke, and he sat down on the platform and asked God to forgive him and save him. He trusted Jesus Christ twenty-some feet in the air.

Suddenly, the lights in the pool area came on. The attendant had come in to check the pool. As Charles looked down from his platform he saw an empty pool, which had been drained for repairs. He had almost plummeted to his death, but the cross had stopped him from disaster.

For the message of the cross is foolishness to those who are perishing, but to us who are being saved it is the power of God.

1 CORINTHIANS 1:18

My Friend Mandy

NANCIE CARMICHAEL

andy and I had been best friends since we were little, in kinder-garten. We did everything together—took piano lessons from the same teacher, played on the same soccer team, went to the same church. Our parents were friends, and we were back and forth at each other's houses lots of times for sleepovers. We told each other everything and pinky-swore that we would never betray one another. People would smile when they saw us coming, "There's those twins—Mandy and Lindsey!"

On lazy summer afternoons, we would sit up in the tree house her dad made for her and her brother, eat cherry Popsicles, and dream about what we were going to be when we grew up. We wanted to go to the same college, get jobs in a city somewhere, and share an apartment. And when we both met the gorgeous guys we would fall madly in love with, we would be in each other's weddings.

But when we got to high school, things started to change between Mandy and me. It started our freshman year, when I went out for volleyball and made the team. Mandy didn't even want to try. We got to travel to some away games, and it was a lot of fun, especially getting to know my new friend, Shelley, one of the best players on the team. Shelley was great at giving me tips on some of the volleyball plays as it was the first year for me.

Shelley had a wacky sense of humor and was one of the popular kids. She and I hit it off right away as we both liked music. The boys really liked her too—she had long blond hair and wore the neatest clothes. She had a knack for putting outfits together and looking great without looking too fixed up. I found myself trying to copy some of the ways she dressed.

It was special having a friend like Shelley. I was starting to notice some of the boys, but I was so self-conscious that I was terrified I'd say or do the wrong thing when they were around. But I'd walk down the hall and Shelley would see me coming. "Hey Lindsey-babes!" she'd call, "What's goin' on?" As I hung out around her locker, the boys would gather, and she took me right into her circle. I felt safe with her, and it was exciting, like I was growing up now for sure. I could tell some of the guys were checking me out, too, and with Shelley I felt more confident.

Her group wasn't the kind I was used to hanging out with—none of them were from my youth group, and I'd heard conversations about some of the parties they'd gone to, but I thought I could handle it.

But back to Mandy. We'd always had lunch together at school. Always. We'd find each other at noon and sit down and check to see what we had in our lunch, or we'd buy something in the cafeteria. Sometimes we'd each have a friend or two with us, and after we sat down, we'd said a quick prayer together before we ate. The prayer helped us support each other in our Christian walks at school. So it had always been Mandy and me at lunch. And it was that way forever until that afternoon Shelley and I were riding the bus home from a volleyball game. Shelley asked, "Lindsey, what's the deal with Mandy?"

"Mandy? Oh, we've known each other since kindergarten."

"Yeah? How come she's so…you know, *quiet?*"

I laughed. "What do you mean, quiet? She's just Mandy."

Shelley said, "Listen, Lindsey. You have real cool-potential. The guys think you're hot, I can tell. But you've got to shake free of those loser-people you're hanging out with at lunch. So how about it—tomorrow, I'm saving you a place at my table. Got it?"

"Yeah, sure," I said, but my heart was pounding. Mandy, a loser? I started thinking about Mandy, and I began to see her the way Shelley saw her: stringy brown hair that she never knew quite how to manage, thick glasses. And Mandy was still dressing like a kid. Sometimes she wore the same thing two days in a row, like she couldn't care less what she put on. And until you got to know Mandy, you didn't know how fun she could be, or that even though she was quiet sometimes, when she said something you could tell she'd been thinking about it. But all of a sudden I realized the awful truth: *Mandy was a geek.* And I was her best friend.

That day I began to understand some of the rules of the game: Cool kids don't come to the geek table. And you might say a brief "Hi" to somebody, but there were unwritten rules that were stronger than anything. And Shelley was letting me know that Mandy could keep me from being popular. I never told anybody what Shelley said to me about Mandy, but I thought about it. I decided I couldn't just ditch Mandy—we'd been friends too long—but it was true that I needed to branch out a little. *Maybe I'm just out-growing Mandy,* I reasoned. *It's good for both of us to have new friends, being in high school and all.*

So that year I started to eat at Shelley's table. I'd tell Mandy, "Shelley and I need to talk about volleyball," or make up some excuse like that. "I'll call you when I get home, Mandy." I could tell Mandy was a little hurt, but I would call her when I got home, because after all, she was still my best friend. My oldest friend, anyway. "Well okay, Linz," she'd say. "We'll do stuff together when volleyball season's over." We'd see each other in the hallway at school and sometimes she'd start to come over but I'd quickly say "Hey, Mandy," and move off to find my new friends. I could see the hurt and bewilderment in her eyes and I felt bad, but how could I explain it to her?

And when we were at church or youth group, we still sat together like we were best friends. But when we were at school, it was different, and after a while, it seemed like she accepted the fact that at school, she went her way and I went mine. It went on like this for a year and a half, and things were going great for me at school. I was elected vice president of my class, and Shelley was elected president. Now Shelley and I had even more in common. Mandy still hung out with the same nerdy bunch—she still didn't do anything to fix herself up, and she still was quiet Mandy. Almost invisible.

We did have a biology class together, though, and Shelley was in the class, too. Shelley and I usually sat in the back of the classroom but Mandy had to sit up front because her eyes were so bad. The teacher, Mr. Larson, was famous for being tough. But worse than that, he was really big on Darwin and the theory of evolution. I'd grown up being taught that God was the Creator and that the world hadn't just happened; there was a wonderful plan that we were all part of. And I really believed it, too. I could never just look at the sky and the beautiful world around me and think that it just happened. I knew deep down in my gut that God made the world, and He made me, too. But I was going to try to get through Mr. Larson's class without making too many waves. I had to get my grade, after all.

Then there was that morning that Mandy totally shocked me. Mr. Larson had some charts up front showing the theory of how man had evolved from apes, and he was going on and on about it. All of a sudden I saw Mandy in front, sitting up straight, her hand raised. "Yes, Mandy?" Mr. Larson said.

"Mr. Larson, I've been doing some reading and studying about this, and what you're teaching is a theory, not fact."

Mr. Larson was sarcastic. "Well, go ahead, Miss Mandy, tell us what's fact."

My heart was thudding. *Oh Mandy, how embarrassing. Don't make a fool of yourself.* I kept my eyes on my notebook, doodling.

"Well, there are many scientists today who agree with the Bible's teaching that God created the world, created people," Mandy said hesitatingly, and then as Mr. Larson waited, she went on, her voice getting stronger. "The fact is that there have never been fossils discovered that evolved outside the species. And besides, Mr. Larson, just the amazing things I've heard you teach in this class is enough to make me believe this whole world couldn't have just happened. There has to be a plan behind it." I stole a look at Mr. Larson, but instead of being annoyed with her, he had a thoughtful look on his face.

"Thank you, Mandy," he said. "What you are saying is very valid. Do any of the rest of you have anything to say?" And then you wouldn't believe what happened—it was incredible. A lot of kids started talking about what a miracle creation was, and how they agreed with Mandy, and we got into a really interesting discussion. Except for me, of course. I kept my mouth shut. Before long, the bell rang and it was time for lunch.

I just sat in back of the room, looking at my friend Mandy. She was up in the front of the room with Mr. Larson and four or five kids, and they were laughing and talking and all of a sudden I realized what an idiot I'd been. What was that look on Mr. Larson's face—and the other kids' faces, too, as they talked to Mandy? It was *respect*. I felt sick to my stomach and knew that in the long run, respect was a whole lot better than being popular.

The truth is, Mandy was being true to what she knew—and true to her best friend ever—Jesus Christ. Little old, quiet Mandy. I hadn't been true to anybody but my own self—wanting to be accepted at the expense of my friends, my faith. I hoped it wasn't too late for me to make things right with Mandy.

I walked toward the front of the room, and she saw me coming. "Mandy, you were *awesome*," I said, tears in my eyes. We hugged each other as I asked, "Any chance you wanna have lunch with me?"

She grinned and pushed her long brown hair back out of her eyes. "You bet, best buddy," she said, as we turned to go. Then I remembered Shelley, who was standing back, waiting for me with a new look of uncertainty on her face. "Oh Shelley," I said, "We're going to go eat."

Mandy put out her hand. "Why don't you come too, Shelley?" And the three of us walked out together.

Many years later I went back to my high school reunion, and it was great to see my old friends Mandy and Shelley. Mandy had gone on to be a teacher—and a really great one, winning some kind of national award (yes, her hair is still a mess). Shelley became a wife and mother and interior decorator, and best of all, a deeply committed Christian. She still looks disgustingly great and has a bouncy personality. Mandy and Shelley ended up living in the same city and you guessed it—they've become best friends.

Me? I became a wife and mother, and as my own daughter asks me questions about friendship and acceptance I tell her about Mandy, and Shelley, and me.

Planning Ahead

KENNETH BOA
FROM *THAT I MAY KNOW GOD*

Years ago, a minister waited in line to have his car filled with gas just before a long holiday weekend. The attendant worked quickly, but there were many cars ahead of him in front of the service station. Finally, the attendant motioned him toward a vacant pump.

"Reverend," said the young man, "sorry about the delay. It seems as if everyone waits until the last minute to get ready for a long trip." The minister chuckled, "I know what you mean. It's the same in my business."

Praise in the Dugout

GREG GRIFFIN
FROM *STILL MORE HOT ILLUSTRATIONS*
FOR YOUTH TALKS

Orel Herschiser pitched an unbelievable season for the Los Angeles Dodgers. Following a complete game shutout in August, he pitched multiple shutout innings and hurled five more complete games through the end of the regular season. He did not allow his opponents to score an earned run in 59 consecutive innings.

When the Dodgers faced the New York Mets in the National League play-offs, Orel continued to dominate hitters, leading the Dodgers to victory by pitching more than 24 innings, crowned by a complete game shutout in the final game! In the World Series his complete game victory over the Oakland A's in game five clinched the series for the Dodgers. No wonder Orel was awarded the Cy Young award and two Most Valuable Player awards, one for the National League play-offs and the other for the World Series.

During the play-offs, the TV cameras zoomed in on this legend in the making. They caught Orel in the dugout between innings singing softly to himself. Unable to make out the tune, the announcers merely commented that Orel's record certainly gave him something to sing about.

Johnny Carson replayed that tape on the "Tonight Show" a few days later when Orel appeared. Johnny asked him what song he had been singing during the game and if Orel would sing it again right there and then. The audience roared its approval over Orel's embarrassed reluctance.

So on national TV, Orel softly sang the tune TV crews had barely caught on tape:

> *Praise God from whom all blessings flow.*
> *Praise Him all creatures here below;*
> *Praise Him above ye heavenly host,*
> *Praise Father, Son and Holy Ghost. Amen.*

Rachel

SHERI ROSE SHEPHERD
FROM *LIFE IS NOT A DRESS REHEARSAL*
FORMER MRS. UNITED STATES

If you know the Lord Jesus as your Savior, you are a child of the King. Each one of God's children has a royal call on their lives (1 Peter 2:9). I had the privilege of knowing a beautiful young girl who took her reign on earth seriously. She was a true princess who kept divine appointments every day of her life. Her name was Rachel. She went to a public school that was more like a war zone than a place to learn. Drugs were everywhere. Gangs terrorized the students. Godly values were nonexistent.

During her freshman year when she was thirteen, Rachel began to feel tired all the time and lost her appetite. A trip to the doctor brought tragic news: Rachel had leukemia.

The diagnosis left Rachel with a choice: become bitter or better. Rachel had no room for bitterness in her life. "I don't know how long I have to live," she told her parents, "and I know that God can choose to heal me. But I'm going to bring as many people home with me into eternity as I can. I'm committed to making every day count for Jesus." Rachel asked her parents to hold her accountable and pray over her every day before school that God would give her a divine appointment with a schoolmate.

The rumor had spread through her school that she had cancer, so all eyes were on her every day. This trial gave Rachel a chance to show her classmates the peace and joy only God can bring in such a tragic situation. In a way, she was blessed in her affliction because she could grasp more intently the truth that our days are numbered. In the Bible, Peter reminds us that we are strangers and aliens in this place. We are only visitors.

The kids at school could not understand why, even though she was dying, Rachel was so concerned about them. She shared the love of Christ with everyone she could. On her sixteenth birthday, she told her parents, "I'm ready to go home and be with the Lord now. I just want to bring my high school with me." That night, she wrote a letter to her school. A few weeks later, Rachel answered God's call to be with Him in heaven.

Rachel's mother asked the principal if her daughter's classmates could come to the funeral to hear the letter Rachel wrote. It was only when the principal announced Rachel's funeral that the full impact of her three years of evangelism became clear. Hundreds of students requested permission to go, and a fleet of school buses carried them from the campus to the funeral. I was in the enormous crowd as the pastor began to read: "Dear Classmates: I told my parents that I was willing to die and go home into eternity if I could bring all of you with me. My Savior made a way for you to get to the other side...."

After the letter was finished, the pastor looked up and asked, "How many of you want to see Rachel someday on the other side of eternity?" Almost every student in the room surged forward to give their lives to Jesus Christ.

How many of those kids will grow up to be godly parents? How many will become pastors, teachers, and evangelists? Because one princess understood she had a royal call on her life and kept her divine appointments, she changed people's lives for eternity.

I challenge you today: when you've gone to be with Jesus, what will you be remembered for? What do you want to be remembered for? Life is not a dress rehearsal. When it's over, it's over. Live this day as if it's your last, and watch what happens to you and everyone around you.

Ellie and Rolf

REBECCA MANLEY PIPPERT
FROM *A HEART LIKE HIS*

hroughout history God's people have been willing to pay the price for truth and loyalty. A gray-haired woman of sixty with a heavy German accent spoke to a congregation in Tennessee. She was a Jew who had been captured as a teenager and sent to prison camp during the Second World War. Her story was not unlike others of the tragic suffering of prisoners inside German concentration camps.

After months of abuse and malnutrition that led to starvation, she realized that if she had any hope of escaping she had to do it while she still had some strength. Having just graduated from high school, she saw women just a few years older than she was who already looked elderly. She plotted an escape carefully and tried to leave no detail to chance.

On the night of her escape she had maneuvered every challenge successfully. There was only one hurdle left—a literal one. She had to scale a barbed wire fence to get outside the compound. She was halfway up the fence when the S.S. guard on duty spotted her. He screamed for her to stop, and at gunpoint demanded that she drop down. She did, her knees and legs badly bleeding. She began sobbing, realizing that her only hope of escape had just vanished.

But to her astonishment she heard the guard say, "Ellie? Is that you? It can't be possible!" She looked into his face and realized it was Rolf, a fellow classmate who had been her best friend in middle school. They had shared so many secret dreams and aspirations then. But now it was wartime, and they were on opposite sides.

"Oh, Rolf, go ahead and kill me. Please! I have no reason to live! I have lost all hope. Get it over with and let me die now. There's nothing to live for anyway."

"Ellie, you are so wrong. There is everything to live for so long as you know *who* to live for. I'm going to let you go. I'll guard you until you climb the wall and get on the other side. But would you promise me one thing?"

Ellie looked at him incredulously, thinking he must be joking, but she could see his intensity and knew he meant every word. "What is it, Rolf?" she asked.

"Promise me when you get on the other side and become free, that you will ask one question continuously until someone answers it for you. Ask, 'Why does Jesus Christ make life worth living?' Promise me, Ellie! He's the only reason to live. Promise me you'll ask until you get the answer."

"Yes, I promise, I promise!" she shouted. As she furiously climbed the fence she felt guilty. *I would have said anything*, she thought to herself, *to get out of this hellhole.*

As she dropped to the other side into freedom, she heard several deafening shots. She turned to look as she ran, convinced that Rolf had changed his mind and amazed that his bullets had missed. To her horror, she saw that other S.S. guards, having realized that Rolf allowed and aided her escape, had killed him on the spot. It was as she ran to her freedom that it dawned on her that Rolf died for her that she might know this Jesus. She wondered who this Jesus Christ was, that someone would lay down his own life so that she could know him.

The Incredible Power
of Words

SARAH ADAMS

s I walked through the front door and tossed my school books on the table, I heard my mom say my name. Normally, I would have headed straight to my room to avoid her drunken tirades, but my curiosity got the best of me, and I crept quietly down the hall towards the kitchen to better eavesdrop on this conversation. Mom's back was turned to me, but I could tell by her slurred speech and her unsteady swaying that she'd been drinking most of the afternoon.

That didn't surprise me. What totally shocked me were the words I heard coming out of my mother's mouth. Using terms that would make a sailor blush, my mom ranted and raved into the phone, describing my immoral lifestyle.

Too stunned to even cry, I ran to my room.

Is that really what my own mother thinks of me?

Even though some of my friends had begun experimenting with sex and drugs, I still held fast to the moral standard I'd been raised with—saving myself until marriage. I didn't have a personal relationship with God, but I did have a conscience. Morals mattered to me.

What my mom thought mattered, too, and the wounds from her words went deep. It was hard enough being a "good kid" in a home where alcohol often turned my parents into irrational strangers. But to have my mom think—and speak—such terrible lies about me.... In my pain and confusion, I grimly determined to live up to her expectations

Opportunities to fulfill her bleak prophecies came easily. Drugs dulled my conscience along with my aching heart. Soon, I surpassed all my friends in their rebellious lifestyles. Because of their own alcohol addiction, my parents never even noticed my swift decline...until the day I didn't come home.

"Go home, child."

At first, I thought it was the cold that had awakened me. I lay shivering under my thin shawl on the bare mattress, trying to pull my thoughts together. Then I heard it again, clearly, only not with my ears. I heard with my heart.

"Go home, Sarah."

I instinctively sensed that God was speaking to me, but vaguely wondered why He would tell me to go to the last place on earth I wanted to be. The cold forced me to get up and move, and that's when I first noticed that I was alone. The usual sprawl of unconscious bodies was missing, and as I stumbled about the filthy apartment, I realized that so were my stash, my drug money, and even my clothes. While I'd been sleeping off my latest fix, my "friends" had taken everything I owned and taken off.

Minutes later, I found myself standing in the rain, thumb out, hitching a ride towards home. I had nowhere else to go. Anxiety grew in my heart as each ride brought me closer to the explosive environment I'd escaped. All too quickly, I found myself dropped off at a gas station only miles from my house.

"Oh God, I don't want to go home—help me!"

Only silence answered my prayer. Despondent, I waited in the gray drizzle for the next car to stop. Soaked and shivering, I climbed into the Volkswagen bug that slowed and stopped a few yards past me. The driver was a young man with curly black hair and the kindest blue eyes I'd ever seen. He drove me home that day, but more than that—he pointed me towards heaven.

Before he took me home, he bought me lunch. After devouring the first real food I'd had in days, I found myself pouring out my heart to this total stranger, telling him why I'd run away and why I was even more afraid to go home. He listened quietly until I'd finished talking, then looked directly at me with his piercing eyes.

"Sarah," he said gently, "you are so precious to God. I've just met you, but I can sense your sweet spirit."

Before I could protest, he continued, "God has wonderful plans and a special purpose for your life, and as strange as this may sound, I believe the road to this new life begins by going home."

"Go home, Sarah."

The words from earlier that day came echoing back to my heart. I felt an unexplainable peace—an assurance that everything would work out all right. Even though I had no idea how.

My new friend took me home that day, and I found my parents in worse shape than when I'd left. But God had a plan for me, and I moved in with Christian relatives the following week. My aunt and uncle not only provided a stable home life for me, they took me to their little country church each Sunday. There I sat, week after week, listening to the amazing truth of God's love for me.

The words the young man had spoken to me began to bear fruit. I longed for a relationship with my loving heavenly Father, and wanted to know His plans and purposes for me. One Sunday, I found myself walking down the aisle and left the church a new creature in Christ. I'll never forget how I felt that day—every sin had been washed away! I was pure—I was clean. Forgiven for all I'd done.

And I'll never forget that young man who obeyed the Spirit's prompting and offered hope to me.

Thank you for the ride. And for speaking words of life.

How Can They Believe?

ROMANS 10:14
THE LIVING BIBLE

But how shall they ask him to save them
unless they believe in him?
And how can they believe in him
if they have never heard about him?
And how can they hear about him
unless someone tells them?

True Hero of the Titanic

MOODY ADAMS
FROM *THE TITANIC'S LAST HERO*

John Harper was born to a pair of solid Christian parents on May 29, 1872. It was on the last Sunday of March 1886, when he was thirteen years old, that he received Jesus as the Lord of his life. He never knew what it was to "sow his wild oats." He began to preach about four years later, at the ripe old age of seventeen years old, by going down to the streets of his village and pouring out his soul in earnest entreaty for men to be reconciled to God.

As John Harper's life unfolded, one thing was apparent.... He was consumed by the Word of God. When asked by various ministers what his doctrine consisted of, he was known to reply, "The Word of God!" After five or six years of toiling on street corners preaching the gospel and working in the mill during the day, Harper was taken in by Reverend E. A. Carter of Baptist Pioneer Mission in London, England. This set Harper free to devote his whole time and energy to the work so dear to his heart. Soon, John Harper started his own church in September of 1896 (now known as the Harper Memorial Church). This church, which John Harper had started with just 25 members, had grown to over 500 members when he left thirteen years later. During this time he had gotten married, but was widowed shortly thereafter. However brief the marriage, God did bless John Harper with a beautiful little girl named Nana.

Ironically, John Harper almost drowned several times during his life. When he was two and a half years of age, he almost drowned when he fell into a well, but was resuscitated by his mother. At the age of twenty-six, he was swept out to sea by a reverse current and barely survived, and at thirty-two, he faced death on a leaking ship in the Mediterranean. Perhaps God used these experiences to prepare this servant for what he faced next.

It was the night of April 14, 1912. The RMS Titanic sailed swiftly on the bitterly cold ocean waters heading unknowingly into the pages of history. On board this luxurious ocean liner were many rich and famous people. At the time of the ship's launch, it was the world's largest man-made, moveable object. At 11:40 P.M. on that fateful night, an iceberg scraped the ship's starboard side, showering the decks with ice and ripping open six watertight compartments. The sea poured in.

On board the ship that night were John Harper and his much beloved six-year-old daughter, Nana. According to documented reports, as soon as it was apparent that the ship was going to sink, John Harper immediately took his daughter to a lifeboat. It is reasonable to assume that this widowed preacher could have easily gotten on board this boat to safety, however, it never seems to have crossed his mind. He bent down and kissed his precious little girl. Looking into her eyes, he told her that she would see him again someday. The flares going off in the dark sky above reflected the tears on his face as he turned and headed toward the crowd of desperate humanity still on the sinking ocean liner. As the rear of the huge ship began to lurch upwards, it was reported that Harper was seen making his way up the deck yelling "Women, children, and unsaved into the lifeboats!" It was only minutes later that the Titanic began to rumble deep within. Most people thought it was an explosion; actually the gargantuan ship was literally breaking in half. At this point, many people jumped off the decks and into the icy, dark waters below. John Harper was one of these people.

That night 1528 people went into the frigid waters. John Harper was swimming frantically to people in the water leading them to Jesus before the hypothermia became fatal. Mr. Harper swam up to one young man who had climbed up on a piece of debris. Reverend Harper asked him between breaths, "Are you saved?" The young man replied that he was not.

Harper then tried to lead him to Christ only to have the young man, who was near shock, reply no. John Harper then took off his lifejacket and threw it to the man and said, "Here then, you need this more than I do..." and swam away to other people. A few minutes later Harper swam back to the young man and succeeded in leading him to salvation. Of the 1528 people that went into the water that night, six were rescued by the lifeboats. One of them was this young man on the debris. Four years later, at a survivors meeting, this young man stood up and in tears recounted how that after John Harper had led him to Christ, Mr. Harper had tried to swim back to help other people, but because of the intense cold had grown too weak to swim. His last words before going under in the frigid waters were, "Believe on the Name of the Lord Jesus, and you will be saved."

Does Hollywood remember this man? No. Oh well, no matter. This servant of God did what he had to do. While other people were trying to buy their way into the lifeboats and selfishly trying to save their own lives, John Harper gave up his life so that others could be saved.

John Harper was truly the hero of the Titanic.

At just the right time, when we were still powerless,
Christ died for the ungodly.
Very rarely will anyone die for a righteous man,
though for a good man someone might possibly dare to die.
But God demonstrates his own love for us in this:
While we were still sinners, Christ died for us.

ROMANS 5:6–8

Thanks for the Bread

MAX LUCADO
FROM *IN THE EYE OF THE STORM*

ear Friend,
    I'm writing to say thanks. I wish I could thank you personally, but I don't know where you are. I wish I could call you, but I don't know your name. If I knew your appearance, I'd look for you, but your face is fuzzy in my memory. But I'll never forget what you did.

There you were, leaning against your pickup in the West Texas oil field. An engineer of some sort. A supervisor on the job. Your khakis and clean shirt set you apart from us roustabouts. In the oil field pecking order, we were at the bottom. You were the boss. We were the workers. You read the blueprints. We dug the ditches. You inspected the pipe. We laid it. You ate with the bosses in the shed. We ate with each other in the shade.

Except that day.

I remember wondering why you did it.

We weren't much to look at. What wasn't sweaty was oily. Faces burnt from the sun; skin black from the grease. It didn't bother me, though. I was there only for the summer. A high-school boy earning good money laying pipe. For me, it was a summer job. For the others, it was a way of life. Most were illegal immigrants from Mexico. Others were drifters, bouncing across the prairie as rootless as tumbleweeds.

We weren't much to listen to, either. Our language was sandpaper coarse. After lunch, we'd light the cigarettes and begin the jokes. Someone always had a deck of cards with lacy-clad girls on the back. For thirty minutes in the heat of the day, the oil patch became Las Vegas—replete with foul language, dirty stories, blackjack, and barstools that doubled as lunch pails.

In the middle of such a game, you approached us. I thought you had a job for us that couldn't wait another few minutes. Like the others, I groaned when I saw you coming.

You were nervous. You shifted your weight from one leg to the other as you began to speak.

"Uh, fellows," you started.

We turned and looked up at you.

"I, uh, I just wanted, uh, to invite..."

You were way out of your comfort zone. I had no idea what you might be about to say, but I knew that it had nothing to do with work.

"I just wanted to tell you that, uh, our church is having a service tonight and..."

"What?" I couldn't believe it. "He's talking church? Out here? With us?"

"I wanted to invite any of you to come along."

Silence. Screaming silence. The same silence you'd hear if a nun asked a madam if she could use the brothel for a mass. The same silence you'd hear if an Internal Revenue Agent invited the Mafia to a seminar on tax integrity.

Several guys stared at the dirt. A few shot glances at the others. Snickers rose just inches from the surface.

"Well, that's it. Uh, if any of you want to go...uh, let me know."

After you turned and left, we turned and laughed. We called you "reverend," "preacher," and "the pope." We poked fun at each other, daring one another to go. You became the butt of the day's jokes.

I'm sure you knew that. I'm sure you went back to your truck knowing the only good you'd done was to make a good fool out of yourself. If that's what you thought, then you were wrong.

That's the reason for this letter.

I thought of you this week. I thought of you when I read about someone else who took a risk at lunch. I thought of you when I read the story of the little boy who gave his lunch to Jesus.

His lunch wasn't much. In fact, it wasn't anything compared to what was needed for more than five thousand people.

He probably wrestled with the silliness of it all. What was one lunch for so many? He probably asked himself if it was even worth the effort.

How far could one lunch go?

I think that's why he didn't give the lunch to the crowd. Instead he gave it to Jesus. Something told him that if he would plant the seed, God would grant the crop.

So he did.

He summoned his courage, got up off the grass, and walked into the circle of grownups. He was as out of place in that cluster as you were in ours. He must have been nervous. No one likes to appear silly.

Someone probably snickered at him, too.

If they didn't snicker, they shook their heads. "The little fellow doesn't know any better."

If they didn't shake their heads, they rolled their eyes. "Here we have a hunger crisis, and this little boy thinks that a sack lunch will solve it."

But it wasn't the men's heads or eyes that the boy saw; he saw only Jesus.

You must have seen Jesus, too, when you made your decision. Most people would have considered us to be unlikely deacon material. Most would have saved their seeds for softer soil. And they'd have been almost right. But Jesus said to give...so you gave.

As I think about it, you and the little boy have a lot in common:

You both used your lunch to help others.

You both chose faith over logic.

You both brought a smile to your Father's face.

There's one difference, though. The boy got to see what Jesus did with his gift, and you didn't. That's why I'm writing. I want you to know that at least one of the seeds fell into a fertile crevice.

Some five years later, a college sophomore was struggling with a decision. He had drifted from the faith given to him by his parents. He wanted to come back. He wanted to come home. But the price was high. His friends might laugh. His habits would have to change. His reputation would have to be overcome.

Could he do it? Did he have the courage?

That's when I thought of you. As I sat in my dorm room late one night, looking for the guts to do what I knew was right, I thought of you.

I thought of how your love for God had been greater than your love for your reputation.

I thought of how your obedience had been greater than your common sense.

I remembered how you had cared more about making disciples than about making a good first impression. And when I thought of you, your memory became my motivation.

So I came home.

I've told your story dozens of times to thousands of people. Each time the reaction is the same: The audience becomes a sea of smiles, and heads bob in understanding. Some smile because they think of the "clean-shirted engineers" in their lives. They remember the neighbor who brought the cake, the aunt who wrote the letter, the teacher who listened.

Others smile because they have done what you did. And they, too, wonder if their "lunchtime loyalty" was worth the effort.

You wondered that. What you did that day wasn't much. And I'm sure you walked away that day thinking that your efforts had been wasted.

They weren't.

So I'm writing to say thanks. Thanks for the example. Thanks for the courage. Thanks for giving your lunch to God. He did something with it; it became the Bread of Life for me.

Gratefully,
Max

P.S. If by some remarkable coincidence you read this and remember that day, please give me a call. I owe you lunch.

Jesus said, "I am the bread of life.
No one who comes to me will ever be hungry again.
Those who believe in me will never thirst."

JOHN 6:35
NEW LIVING TRANSLATION

A Pirate from the House of Prayer

VOICE OF THE MARTYRS
FROM *JESUS FREAKS*

he young woman stood on the corner handing out small cards with poems on them. Some took them because they were interested in what she might be handing out, some because she was incredibly beautiful, but most probably took the cards because of the joy and love that shone in her smile as she looked each person in the eye and handed them a card. Each card contained a poem she had written herself. Each poem declared the love and joy she had from knowing Jesus as Lord and Savior.

For this she was arrested and brought to trial. Before the court she boldly testified, "The society which you, the Communists, are building can never be just because you yourselves are unjust." She was sentenced to one year imprisonment.

When she was released, she went straight back to her work for the underground church. Because of her beauty, determination, and boldness, she was labeled "a pirate from the house of prayer" by the Communist newspaper *Izvestia*.

One of the things she dared to write was, "You, the atheists, can meet together at any time and do whatever you like—talk, read, or sing. Why, then, can we not pray or read the Bible whenever we want? We are allowed to speak about God only in church. You would certainly not acquiesce if you were allowed to talk about the theater only in a theater or about books only in a library. *In the same way, we cannot be silent about what constitutes the whole meaning of our life—about Christ.*" Again she was arrested and this time was sentenced to four years in prison, but she did not waver.

By the age of 27, Aida was facing her fourth prison term, yet prison seemed to do little but increase her love for God's Word and its importance to her faith. "If it were the other way around, that we had a plentiful supply of Bibles and that there were none in England, I'd be prepared to be the first to take Bibles there.... In prison, the most difficult thing was to live without a Bible.

Once, a gospel of Mark was smuggled in to her. "When the guards learned that I had a gospel, they became alarmed and searched the whole camp. During the second search, they found it. I was punished for this and had to spend ten days and ten nights in solitary confinement in a cold cell. But two weeks later I was given a whole New Testament which I was able to keep almost until the day of my release.

"The prison was searched many times, but each time the Lord helped me. I knew in advance about the search and was able to keep the precious book. Many other prisoners helped me hide the book, even though they were not Christians."

The guards did many other things to try to discourage her and make her deny her faith, but some of these backfired on them. "Once the guard showed me a food parcel. He told me that it contained chocolate and other good things. It was not given to me, but it was an encouragement to know that my friends cared about me. That fact meant much more than the food. On another occasion, I was told ten packages had arrived for me from Norway, but I was not given these either...*It is a great joy for us to experience definite spiritual fellowship with Christians in different parts of the world. This gave us hope in prison.* I want to send an expression of love from us all to those who have cared about us and prayed for us."

When she was released from her fourth term, Aida had changed drastically. The movie-star beauty of her youth was not only gone, but at only thirty years of age she looked more than fifty. She was haggard and worn by the years of imprisonment. If you had seen her, you would never have recognized her as the same woman, except for one thing: her smile. It still reflected the love and joy of knowing Jesus as Lord and Savior.

Of her last and hardest term in prison, Aida wrote, "One text became clearer than ever before, 'My yoke is easy, my burden is light' (Matthew 11:30). Jesus himself spoke these words and during the three years of prison I came to understand how real and true they are."

Hope

Hope itself is like a star—not to be seen

in the sunshine of prosperity,

and only to be discovered

in the night of adversity.

—CHARLES SPURGEON

Daughter of the King

Sheri Rose Shepherd
from *Life is Not a Dress Rehearsal*
Former Mrs. United States

I had just finished speaking in New York City on the royal call in 1 Peter 2:9, which says we are God's special people, a royal priesthood who "may proclaim the excellencies of Him who has called you out of darkness into His marvelous light."

"If we pray for a divine appointment to share the gospel every day," I said confidently, "God will give us one."

The pastor of the church where I spoke, along with his wife, spent the next day sightseeing with my husband Steve and me. Before we started out, the pastor suggested, "Let's pray for one of those divine appointments you've been talking about."

What a great idea, I thought. *This is the Big Apple. There certainly couldn't be a shortage of hurting people here.*

We prayed and then set out to make the rounds of all the famous tourist attractions. We saw the Statue of Liberty, drank tea at the Plaza Hotel, ice-skated at Rockefeller Center, and saw the World Trade Center. But as the sun set over the Jersey shore, not a single door had been opened for a divine appointment.

I was getting ready to trip someone so I could pick them up, apologize, and tell them about Jesus. I kept waiting and praying and looking for an opportunity to tell somebody—anybody—about the Lord. I wondered to myself if God had heard our prayer that morning. It would look really bad if I taught this message about sharing the Word of God every day and then didn't follow through.

About 10:00 P.M. we stopped in a coffee shop for a bite to eat before heading back to the pastor's house for the night. Two beautiful young girls came in after we did and sat at the next table. We were near the theater district, and one of the girls walked up to me and said, "Are you a celebrity?"

Recognizing my cue I said, "Yes. I am a daughter of the King. My Father created the heavens and the earth."

Finally my appointment had showed up. The two girls looked at each other, then back at me. "What does that mean?" the other one asked.

"You know that God created the heavens and the earth?" I asked.

"Yes," she answered.

"Well, Jesus is my Savior," I explained. "So that means I have a relationship with God, and that makes me His daughter. My God is the King of kings and Lord of lords."

We talked with the two girls all the way through their dinner. Under any other circumstances, I would have excused myself and attacked my caesar salad. But they were listening so intently, I forgot all about it.

"Well," one of the girls said after half an hour, "I could never accept this Jesus and become a daughter of the King because I'm Jewish."

"What a coincidence!" I exclaimed. "So is my Savior. And so am I." I shared my testimony with the girls, and Steve shared Scriptures with them about God's eternal plan for their lives. As I was going over all that God had done in my life—how He had delivered me out of drug abuse, bulimia, a broken heart, and a broken home—one of the girls started to cry.

"I just got out of a drug rehab program last week," she said. "Say, are you guys angels?"

"No," I answered, "but we are messengers, and this is the divine appointment we prayed for this morning. You see, God arranged for us to meet you here today so that we could give you a message of hope and eternal life. And now we would love to invite you to become daughters of the King yourselves and receive the eternal crown, so that you can experience

God's peace in your life today and enjoy His presence for all eternity."

Right there in the restaurant, those two girls accepted Jesus as their savior and became daughters of the King. What a wonderful, glorious day it was! How different the story would have been if all Steve and I had had to talk about was how rude New Yorkers are, how expensive the food is, and how much our feet hurt. Every day, our steps are ordered of the Lord, and our conversation can cause people to thirst for righteousness in Christ.

As Mrs. United States I won a crown and banner. But infinitely more important, I have a crown that is eternal, a banner that is God's love, and the privilege of wearing the name of Jesus on my heart always. Never stop looking for the divine appointment He has waiting for you every day of the year, every year of your life.

making a
difference

Full Circle

I used to ask God to help me.
Then I asked if I might help Him.
I ended up asking Him to do His work through me.

HUDSON TAYLOR

Chris's Legacy

ANDY STANLEY
FROM *VISIONEERING*

hris had a vision. His vision was to share the gospel with every student at Dunwoody High School. Chris first let me know about his vision at the beginning of his senior year. He and I met together on Tuesday afternoons for discipleship. As his youth pastor, I was both thrilled and humbled. Thrilled at his zeal. Humbled by memories of my senior year. I don't know about you, but my senior year "visions" were not what you would consider positive illustration material. Anyway Chris told me about his vision, and we went to work trying to figure out a way to make it happen.

One of our obstacles was that Chris was not what you would consider a mainstream kind of guy. He wasn't the president of anything. He wasn't on any teams. He didn't date a cheerleader. He wasn't an honor student. He didn't even dress like everybody else. Chris was a skater.

Now in certain communities around Atlanta, being a skater would put you in one of the top echelons in your local junior high or high school. But not at Dunwoody. At Dunwoody High, skaters got no respect. There weren't that many to begin with. And the handful that were there were alternative before alternative was cool. Bottom line, Chris wasn't going to be asked to speak to the student body in this lifetime. He had no leverage. All he had was a vision.

But Chris wasn't discouraged. He felt this was something God would have him pursue. He felt it was his responsibility to make sure everybody in his school had at least one opportunity to hear a clear gospel presentation once before he or she graduated. So we explored every option imaginable. We thought about writing everybody a letter. We discussed doing a phone blitz. I suggested dropping notes in everybody's locker. But none of these ideas seemed right. The year came and went and Chris's vision never came to fruition—or so it seemed.

Like Nehemiah, however, Chris was faithful to do what he could while trusting God to do what he couldn't. During his senior year, Chris took advantage of every opportunity to share his faith with other students. One of the fellows he had an opportunity to share with was Mark.

Mark grew up with his mom in Miami. His folks had split up when he was younger, and his dad eventually moved to Atlanta. When Mark hit adolescence, he did so with a vengeance. He fell prey to the allurement of alcohol and drugs. He was flunking out of school. By the end of his tenth grade year, his mom had had enough. She packed him up and sent him to Atlanta to live with his dad.

Mark didn't want to leave his friends in Miami. He didn't really want to live with his dad. As far as he was concerned, life...well you get the picture. With that in mind, imagine his first day at Dunwoody High School. He had an attitude that preceded him by about ten minutes everywhere he went. This was not a kid you walked up to and greeted in the hall. Consequently, nobody reached out to Mark. Nobody except, you guessed it, Chris.

One of the most remarkable things about Chris was that nobody intimidated him. He wasn't put off by Mark. He saw him for what he was: an angry, hurt young man in need of a friend and a Savior. So Chris went right up, introduced himself, and showed him around. As it turned out, they both liked some of the same music. In fact, Mark was a drummer and Chris played bass. That weekend, Chris invited Mark to spend the night with him at his parents' house.

At this juncture in Chris's life, he assumed all bets were off with his vision. There was no way he was going to be able to share the gospel with the student body. God hadn't provided a vehicle. The best he could do was get in as many one-on-one exchanges as possible before the year ended.

Little did he know God had not given up on the vision. He was still quietly at work behind the scenes. And Mark was going to play a key role in seeing to it that Chris's vision became a reality.

Late that evening, after several hours of listening to music, Mark opened up with Chris. He told him about his life in Miami. He shared his reluctance about coming to Atlanta. He admitted he was pretty much mad at the world.

When he finished, Chris, a seventeen-year-old high school student, told Mark that he had a heavenly Father who loved him in spite of all he had done. He told him about Christ dying for his sin so he could be forgiven. That night, Mark put his trust in Christ and became a Christian. Then Chris told him about his cool youth pastor (me!) and about his church. The next Sunday Mark showed up. He joined our student ministry.

The school year came and went. Chris graduated and went to college. Meanwhile Mark had one more year of high school. I asked Mark to be in my discipleship class. Through that year we became good friends.

Then one Wednesday night, right before our student Bible study, Mark ran up to me with a look of panic on his face. "Andy, you won't believe it." Mark started every sentence that way. "You won't believe it, I have been asked to speak to the whole student body during our Arrive Alive assembly!"

Every year, on the Friday afternoon just before spring break, Dunwoody High School conducted a campuswide assembly program dedicated to warning students about the dangers of drinking and driving. Typically, they would invite someone who had a gory tale to tell. The stories usually involved a head-on collision, multiple broken bones, and a long hospital stay. Occasionally, the speaker would show a scar or two.

The idea was to motivate students to be careful while they were away on spring break. Often, they would put a car that had been totaled by a drunk driver on the campus lawn as a visual aid.

Well, Mrs. Dolworth, the principal, knew Mark had been heavily involved with alcohol and drugs before coming to her school. Furthermore, she was aware that a remarkable change had taken place in his life. She thought it would be a good idea if Mark, being a student, would follow the featured speaker at the assembly. So she called Mark and asked him to share his story.

"Do you think I should tell them my *whole* story?" he asked.

I smiled. "Mark, when I speak at a public school, they won't even announce where I work. They introduce me as an adolescent counselor. God has given you a unique opportunity. You are a student. You can say anything you want. Yes, I think you ought to tell them your whole story."

I will never forget walking into the gym that Friday afternoon. My heart was pounding so hard I could hear it. I rarely get nervous when I speak. But I was so nervous for Mark I wasn't sure I was going to be able to stay.

The gym was packed. It was literally standing room only. Students, faculty, teachers—they were all there. Mrs. Dolworth introduced their keynote speaker. He had graduated from Dunwoody High several years prior. He did a good job telling his story. Lots of blood and guts. The students loved it. But his conclusion was flat. After thirty minutes of car wrecks and life-threatening injuries, he said, "So students, hang together. You have each other. Thank you." And he sat down.

Everyone clapped politely. Then Mrs. Dolworth walked to the center of the gymnasium and announced, "This afternoon we have one of our own students who is going to share for just a few minutes about some changes that have taken place in his life. Please welcome Mark Hannah."

I thought I was going to die. Mark walked slowly out to center court, took the microphone off the stand and began. "When I first came to Dunwoody High School, I hated everything and everybody." He talked about his life in Miami. He shared about his intense anger. He delved into his experience with alcohol and drugs.

You could have heard a pin drop—except for the fact that my heart was beating so hard I'm sure it must have distracted the people around me.

Then Mark turned the corner. "One day a guy named Chris Folley introduced himself to me and invited me to his house. That night I told him all about my life. I told him how much I hated everybody. He listened. And then he told me Jesus loved me. He explained how He died on the cross for my sins. He said I could be forgiven. That night I prayed with Chris and my life changed.

"Everything hasn't been easy since then. I still have my struggles. But now I don't have to face them alone. If you have any questions about anything I've said, I would be happy to talk with you afterwards. Thank you."

With that, he placed the microphone back in the stand and sauntered back to his assigned place on the bleachers. Meanwhile, the entire student body stood to their feet in applause. They clapped and cheered for what must have been several minutes. It was too much for me. I left the gym and headed for my car.

Strangely enough, it wasn't until I walked outside that the significance of what had just happened hit me. "Lord, this was about Chris, wasn't it?"

Even as I type these words, tears fill my eyes as I think back to one senior in high school who was faithful to do what he could while trusting God to do what he couldn't. Chris's concerns were in alignment with the Father's. So he went to work behind the scenes to ensure that the vision became a reality.

Well done, my good and faithful servant.

MATTHEW 25:21
NEW LIVING TRANSLATION

The Summer That Changed My Life

CARLA BARNHILL
FROM *CAMPUS LIFE* MAGAZINE

as the camp bell rang to signal the start of our next activity, my friend Pam and I raced back to our cabin to change out of our soaking wet clothes. We'd successfully annoyed our cute sailing instructor, Jay, by capsizing our little Sunfish no less than five times in one hour, sort of accidentally on purpose.

Laughing our way up the path to our cabin, we were surprised to see our counselor, Deb, sitting on the steps, waiting for us.

"Carla, I need to talk to you for a minute," she said to me.

"What's up?" I asked.

"Your mom just called. Laurie died this morning," Deb answered.

There was nothing I could say. I just started walking, dazed, as Deb led me to the camp office where I could call my mom.

Laurie was my 13-year-old cousin, just a couple of years younger than me. For the past two years, she'd been fighting cancer. And now she was dead. Even though I knew it would happen, the thought of her being gone forever still hit me hard.

I talked to my mom for a long time. Funeral on Friday. We'll pick you up. I love you honey. Mom's words floated around in my head. I hung up the phone and looked at Deb, who'd been sitting next to me in the office, holding my hand as I listened to my mom.

"Do you feel like going for a walk?" Deb asked.

"Don't we have to go to Bible class?" I replied.

"Don't worry about it," she said.

For the next hour, Deb and I walked through the woods. Sometimes I talked, sometimes she did. Other times, we just walked in silence, Deb listened as I sorted out the mishmash of feelings I couldn't quite understand, hugged me as I cried, and laughed with me as I told her some of the silly things Laurie and I had done together before she got so sick. And she assured me that whenever I needed to talk, she would be there for me.

As we walked back to the cabin, I could tell something in me was changing. I'd been a Christian most my life. I'd gone to church with my family since I could remember. I'd been coming to this Bible camp for years. I knew about God's love for me and Jesus' sacrifice on the cross. But that day in the woods with Deb, I felt the power of God's love for the first time.

Deb didn't do anything amazing. She didn't say anything special. She didn't have a perfect answer to any of my questions about death. Instead, she comforted me, listened to me and cried with me. I knew that's just what Jesus would have done had He been there in the flesh that day. Deb's love for me, her expression of God's love for me, changed the way I thought about my faith. I began to realize that being a Christian wasn't just about living a good life and going to church. Being a Christian was also about reaching out to hurting people.

Deb wasn't the only person to reach out to me that week at camp. As word spread among the staff and campers that I'd lost someone I loved, I found myself surrounded by people who made sure I was all right. For the next few days, my sailing buddy Pam resisted the urge to tip our boat over and we spent our class time floating around the lake, just talking. The recreation director, who'd known my cousin, walked up to me after dinner one night and hugged me. No words, just tears and a shared sense of loss. Even campers I didn't know would stand up in chapel and pray for me and my family.

When Friday, the day of Laurie's funeral arrived, I packed up my stuff and waited with Deb for my parents to pick me up. The rest of the campers would leave on Saturday. I was sorry I had to miss the last day of camp, not because I wanted to hit the beach or the craft shack one more time, but because I wasn't ready to leave the people who'd offered me such comfort all week.

As my parents pulled in to camp, I noticed a few girls from my cabin coming to say goodbye. Soon, a few more people joined them, then a few more. I listened as they said their goodbyes.

"We just wanted you to know we'll be thinking of you today."

"We'll pray for your family."

"Remember how much God loves you."

Crying, I climbed into my parents' car. My mom looked at me through tears of her own and said, "As much as I wanted you home this week, I knew this was the right place for you to be. It looks like God's taken good care of you here."

And she was right. God had taken good care of me at camp. As we drove away, I quietly prayed God would never let me forget what I'd learned that week. And I prayed God would help me show His love to the people in my life back at home.

A couple of years later, I was sitting in my living room, surrounded by friends, family and presents. I'd just graduated from high school and was looking forward to one more laid-back summer before heading off to college. As I took a bite of chocolate cake, the phone rang. It was my friend Lisa. "Hey, you want to be a counselor at Trout Lake Camp with me next week?" she asked. "Yes!!!!!" I screamed into the phone. I'd waited for this chance for years. I was old enough to be a cabin counselor at the same camp that had meant so much to me. I couldn't wait to get there.

One week was definitely not enough for me. The next summer, after my freshman year of college, I headed back to camp, this time to be on the summer staff. While I was excited about spending the whole summer at my favorite place in the world, I was even more excited about having the chance to show God's love to campers, the same way that love had been shown to me.

It didn't take long for me to get that chance. One Sunday, as the new campers arrived for the week, a woman came up to me. She said, "You're going to be the counselor for Amanda, my niece. I just wanted you to know that her father died three months ago and she's still having kind of a hard time."

"Thanks for letting me know," I said.

For most of the week, Amanda seemed to really like being at camp. During the day, she'd be off with a new friend, swimming, canoeing or playing miniature golf. At night, she'd giggle with the rest of the nine-year-old girls in the cabin as I tried to get them settled down to sleep. But one evening, as we were leaving the chapel service, Amanda lingered behind. Before long, she slid quietly into the seat next to me and started to cry. I didn't need to ask what was wrong. I just put my arm around her and held her close. We sat that way for a long time. After a while, she looked up at me, wiped the tears off her cheeks and said, "Thanks." Then she left.

We never talked about what she felt that night. We really didn't need to. It seemed to be enough for Amanda that someone was there to hold her while she cried.

Amanda wasn't the only camper I had the chance to comfort during the summers I worked at camp. And every time a high-school girl came to me to talk about her parents' divorce, or a third-grade boy fought off his homesickness while we shared cookies in the dining hall, I found myself thanking God for putting me there, and for allowing me to share His love with other people. With all the love He's shown me, it's the least I can do.

He comes alongside us when we go through hard times,
and before you know it, he brings us alongside someone else
who is going through hard times so that we can be there
for that person just as God was there for us.

2 Corinthians 1:4
The Message

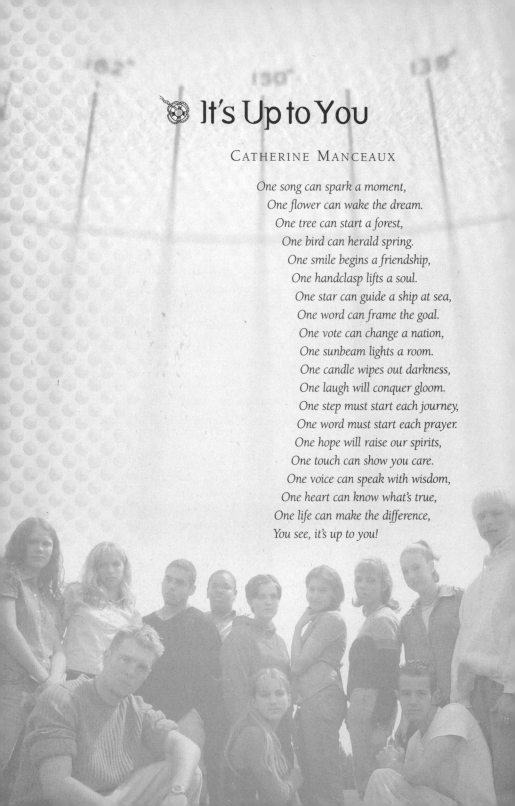

It's Up to You

CATHERINE MANCEAUX

One song can spark a moment,
One flower can wake the dream.
One tree can start a forest,
One bird can herald spring.
One smile begins a friendship,
One handclasp lifts a soul.
One star can guide a ship at sea,
One word can frame the goal.
One vote can change a nation,
One sunbeam lights a room.
One candle wipes out darkness,
One laugh will conquer gloom.
One step must start each journey,
One word must start each prayer.
One hope will raise our spirits,
One touch can show you care.
One voice can speak with wisdom,
One heart can know what's true,
One life can make the difference,
You see, it's up to you!

Bold Faith

SUSIE SHELLENBERGER
FROM *BREAKAWAY* MAGAZINE

eens all over the world are taking strong stands for Jesus Christ. It's not always easy—but it is always rewarding. Here's a true story about three guys who dared to be vocal.

"Hey, Bible Boy. Where's your Word?" shouts a voice from across the crowded hall.

Fifteen-year-old Eric Stueberg grins and holds up a tattered book with fluorescent, lime-green words—HOLY BIBLE—handwritten across the cover.

"Right here," he says. "Wouldn't leave home without it!"

It's Monday morning at Florida's Fort Walton Beach High School, and Eric loves his new reputation. When other guys return from the weekend bragging about how far they've gone with a girl or how much they've had to drink, Eric can't stop boasting about his radical God...and how far Christ can take a life that's fired-up for Him.

It all started a few months back when Eric and some of his church friends realized they had work to do for God—starting with their own lives.

"During one of our revival services at Brownsville Assembly of God, the Lord came and His Spirit poured out on our church. It was amazing," says Eric. "And when the pastor invited people to the altar, my friends and I knew we needed to go forward."

The message from Revelation 3:15—about being lukewarm—had touched a nerve. Eric realized that he wasn't on track with Jesus and that attending church on Sundays and Wednesdays wasn't enough.

"You have to *know* Jesus, " Eric says. "He has to be your best friend—

your Lord.

"I thought about how half my school wasn't saved," Eric continues. "I knew I needed to make a change in my life, then reach out to other teens. I finally stood up and went down to the altar. Everything just broke. It was a real turnaround."

One of the first things Eric and his friend Jill did was to start a Bible study at school. The second—and most important, he says—was to step out as a "walking billboard."

"Some teens wear Christian T-shirts and go to church, but they also spend their weekends partying," Eric says. "I used to be that way too. But I've seen how it can completely ruin a Christian's witness."

Today, he's convinced that if you're claiming to be a Christian, you'd better live like it. After all, being a walking billboard means people will read your life. "I want people to read 'JESUS' when they see me," he says. "That's why I love being called Bible Boy. It's cool."

But being radical for God comes at a cost. Eric lost a few friends who thought he'd become too religious, and he occasionally gets picked on. "Let's not kid ourselves; taking a stand for God is far from easy," Eric says. "But who says following Jesus should be easy?"

The first few weeks were the hardest. But gradually, casual friends began calling him Bible Boy—with a positive tone—and some even visited his campus Bible study. What began as a handful of teens who spent their lunch hour praying now fills up a room.

"This world needs bold Christians," says Eric, "Especially teenagers who are willing to stand in the face of what's popular and say, 'Jesus is the *only* truth, the *only* life, and the *only* way.'"

"I don't want my friends to spend eternity in hell. I can't be selfish. I've got to speak up…and do my part to rock my school for Christ."

And Eric's commitment is making a difference. "Today, I'm not the only 'Bible Boy' at school," he says. "There are a lot of us now. And that's awesome."

Excuse Me,
Is Your Daughter in Trouble?

SHERI ROSE SHEPHERD
FROM *LIFE IS NOT A DRESS REHEARSAL*
FORMER MRS. UNITED STATES

I am not normally one of those people who says, "God spoke to me and told me to tell you something." But one time I had an experience I can't explain any other way. I was seated between two large businessmen on a jam-packed airplane. I pulled out my handy-dandy inflatable neck pillow and scrunched down for a little nap, but I couldn't sleep. I thought I heard the Lord say in my spirit, "The man next to you has a daughter who is in trouble. Talk to him."

I tried to remember if I'd eaten anything recently that hadn't been properly refrigerated. *I am making things up*, I told myself. *No way. God doesn't speak to me in this way. I'm pooped, and I'm going to sleep right now.*

Every time I closed my eyes, I kept getting the same message. "The man next to you has a daughter who is in trouble. Talk to him." The man was sophisticated and elegantly dressed. He had his glasses on, reading *The Wall Street Journal*.

I said to myself, *There is no way I'm going to interrupt this guy while he is reading his paper and say, "Excuse me, is your daughter in trouble?"* I kept trying to fall asleep. It was impossible.

Okay, I reasoned silently, *if this is really God nudging me, I am going to take a chance on totally humiliating myself and ask this perfect stranger about his daughter.*

I turned to the man and said, "Excuse me, is your daughter in trouble?"

For an instant his face had a shocked look as if somebody has just doused him with ice water. Then he put his head back, closed his eyes, and started to sob. He let the paper fall into his lap and took off his reading glasses. His shoulders shook and the tears ran down his face.

As soon as he could speak, he turned to me and said, "How could you possibly know that? I have a daughter who is away at college, and she is in terrible trouble. She was a virgin, and she was raped by one of her employers. Now she's pregnant." No wonder God wouldn't let me take a nap.

"The best thing I know to do, sir," I said, "is to pray. I don't know what I can say to lighten your burden. But I know that when I don't have the words, God does."

He said, "Let's pray."

We prayed for his daughter and his family. We prayed for the employer. We prayed for the baby. When we got off the plane, he called his wife immediately and said, "We need to commit our lives to God! We need to start praying for our daughter, and we need to go back to church!"

Six months later I was speaking in southern California and, to my delight, this same man came to see me. He came up to me and said, "You have no idea how your prayers changed my daughter's life. She kept the baby—she's going to put it up for adoption—and she's going to church. My wife and I have recommitted our lives to God, and we're back at church too."

My airplane conversation was a divine appointment, but I almost slept through it.

Thank You, Lord, for being persistent, for making me bold enough to risk ridicule to share Your message. All I wanted was a nap, but You had a job for me that brought Your healing hand to an entire family. Help me, like Paul, to ask for boldness, and never think I'm too busy, too tired, or too timid to do Your will.

Pray that I'll know what to say and have the courage to say it at the right time.

EPHESIANS 6:19, THE MESSAGE

The Red Purse

LOUISE MOERI

I know we aren't supposed to judge people, but where Kennie Jablonsky was concerned, I found it impossible. I decided he was the wrong person in the wrong kind of work.

I'm a swing-shift nursing supervisor, and it's my job to evaluate workers' performances at Homeland Convalescent Hospital.

Kennie Jablonsky was a new employee, tall and very strong, not bad looking, with his blond hair cut to the collar and dark green eyes. After a few weeks' probation, I had to admit he was clean, punctual, and reasonably efficient. But I just didn't like him.

Kennie Jablonsky looked like a hood. I knew the neighborhood he came from—a cesspool of gangs, drugs, and violence. His language was street talk, his manner wry, his walk springy and controlled like a boxer's, and his expression closed-off like the steel door on a bank vault. He seemed too large and carefully controlling of a powerful will to be able to fit into a highly specialized teamwork of a convalescent hospital.

The vast majority of our patients come to us in the final stages of terminal disease or with the most terminal of all diseases—old age. They come to us crippled, weakened, confused, and defeated, no longer able to function out in the world. Many have lost the faculty of rational thought, a casualty of failing health and a world that often seems brutal and indifferent.

Mary B. was one of those. Attendants call her Mary B. because she was one of four Marys in the west wing. At ninety-four years, Mary B. was as frail as a cobweb. She outlived her husband and sisters, and if she had any children, they had long since abandoned her. She was in almost constant motion as long as she was awake.

Mary B. had an obsession that someone had taken her purse. She searched for it all hours of the day and night. Unless tied to her bed or wheelchair, she would go through the door onto the street, into the men's wards, through the laundry room, and into the kitchen, mindlessly searching and never giving up. When restrained, she wanted her wheelchair in the hallway, where she stopped everyone who came near.

"Can you lend me a comb?" she asked. "I've lost mine. It was in my red purse. My money is gone, too. Where is my purse? Where is my purse?"

Every day it was the same, until Mary B.'s queries became background noise, like the sound of hot carts loaded with trays rumbling down the halls, the hum of air conditioning, or the static of the intercom.

We all knew Mary didn't have a purse. But on occasion someone would stop to listen to her out of kindness and concern, although he or she was furiously busy. Still, most of us maneuvered around her with, "Sure, Mary, if I see your purse I'll bring it back."

Most of us—but one.

The last thing I expected of Kennie Jablonsky was that he would listen to Mary B., but, strangely, he always had a word for her.

What is he up to? I wondered, watching him. My first suspicion was that he might be working here to steal drugs. I thought I had spotted a potential troublemaker.

Every day, as Mrs. B. stopped him to ask about her purse, and as Kennie promised to look for it, my suspicions grew. Finally I concluded that Kennie was planning something involving Mary. He's going to steal drugs, I told myself, and somehow hide them around Mary. Then some accomplice will come in and sneak them out of the hospital. I was so sure of all this that I set up more security systems around the drug dispensing department.

One afternoon, just before supper, I saw Kennie walking down the hall with a plastic grocery bag in his hand. It was heavy.

This is it, I told myself, scrambling from behind my desk. I started after him, but realized I needed more evidence. I halted behind a laundry cart, piled high with baskets. It was tall enough to conceal me, but I still could see Kennie clearly as he strode down the hall toward Mary B. in her wheelchair.

He reached Mary and suddenly turned, looking over his shoulder. I dodged out of sight, but I could still see him peering up and down the hall. It was clear he didn't want anyone to see what he was doing.

He raised the bag. I froze…until he pulled out a red purse.

Mary's thin old hands flew up to her face in a gesture of wonder and joy, then flew out hungrily. Like a starved child taking bread, Mary B. grabbed the red purse. She held it for a moment, just to see it, then pressed it to her breast, rocking it like a baby.

Kennie turned and glanced sharply all around. Satisfied no one was watching, he leaned over, unsnapped the flap, reached in and showed Mary a red comb, small coin purse, and a pair of children's toy spectacles. Tears of joy were pouring down Mary's face. At least, I guessed they were. Tears streaked my face, too.

Kennie patted Mary lightly on the shoulder, crumpled the plastic grocery bag, threw it into the nearby waste can, then went about his work down the hall.

I walked back to my desk, sat down, reached into the bottom drawer, and brought out my battered old Bible. Turning to the seventh chapter of Matthew, I asked the Lord to forgive me.

At the end of the shift, I stood near the door used by the aides coming to and from work. Kennie came bouncing down the hall carrying his coat and radio.

"Hi, Kennie," I said. "How's everything going? Do you think you'll like this job?"

Kennie looked surprised, then shrugged. "It's the best I'll ever get," he grunted.

"Nursing is a good career," I ventured. An idea was growing. "Uh, have you ever thought of going on to college for a registered nursing degree?"

Kennie snorted. "Are you kidding? I ain't got a chance for anything like that. The nurse's aide course was free or I wouldn't have *this* job."

I knew this was true. Kennie set down his radio and pulled on his coat. "Take a miracle for me to go to college," he said. "My old man's in San Quentin and my old lady does cocaine."

I clenched my teeth but still smiled. "Miracles do happen," I told him. "Would you go to college if I could find a way to help you with the money?"

Kennie stared at me. All at once the hood vanished, and I caught a glimpse of what could be. "Yes!" was all he said. But it was enough.

"Good night, Kennie," I said as he reached for the door handle. "I'm sure something can be worked out."

I was sure, too, that in Room 306 of the west wing, Mary B. was sleeping quietly, both her arms wrapped around a red purse.

So encourage each other
and build each other up,
just as you are already doing.

1 Thessalonians 5:11
New Living Translation

Four Words

JIM BURNS AND GREG MCKINNON
FROM *ILLUSTRATIONS, STORIES AND QUOTES*
FOR *YOUTH WORKERS*

a young boy wrote a letter to Mother Teresa. He asked her how he could make a difference with his life, like she had with hers. For months, he didn't hear anything from her. Then one day he received a letter from Calcutta, India. He expectantly opened it up and read four words that changed his life. "Find your own Calcutta."

Courage That Changed the World

SANDY AUSTIN

Columbine. Teenagers running with hands on their heads like criminals. Patrick Ireland being pulled from the second story window. The SWAT team in riot gear. Memorial flowers, teddy bears, and signs at Clement Park. The crosses for the victims. We all remember where we were when the news broke of the tragedy at Columbine. That one word, "Columbine," represents tragedy, despair, and fear. Yet the strongest impression I have of it is courage. As a counselor on the scene the day of the shootings and in working with students and parents for six months afterwards, the courage of the young people is what stands out to me.

Cassie Bernall and Valeen Schnurr boldly proclaimed their faith in God while looking down the barrels of the killers' guns. Students stayed in the science room with their teacher Dave Sanders, trying to save his life. More than seventy students crammed in the office of the choir room for several hours, while others huddled in the science lab hearing the killers bragging three feet away on the other side of the door. Were they going to be the next victims?

Students risked their lives dodging the killers' line of fire to pull their friends to safety. A student sprinted for the door with bullets flying past his head while the window of the door exploded in his face. Wounded students in the library, with tears flooding their eyes, hung on for life and endured for three hours the shrill of the fire alarm and water pouring out from the sprinkler system that was set off by the bombs. With their friends' bodies lying next to them, they waited and wondered if help would ever come.

The day after the shootings courage was spreading. At the crisis drop-in center, several from a church youth group waited to get final word about one of their friends. Cassie Bernall. Kara, one of the girls waiting, told of how "this friend" had impacted her life and was her role model. When Kara got final word that Cassie was a victim she was devastated. She clung to her friends while we shared scripture and prayed. Kara said she was going to dedicate her life to keeping her faith in God strong, which is what Cassie lived and died for.

Two weeks later, young people from a group called the "Revival Generation" put on a five-hour outreach for the teenagers in the community at a local church. It was completely planned and hosted by students—no adults were allowed—except for those of us who were available for counseling issues. My heart was stirred by a sight that I will never forget. At the end of the evening a young man—about sixteen—came out of the auditorium walking with a cane. He had three buddies with him. He had an injured leg, and it was obvious that he was very athletic. He was in great shape physically, yet the shooters' bullets forever changed his life. He was gasping for strength as he got closer to the door. Then one of his friends asked for his cane, and another crouched down in front of him. Swinging his arms to help, it took about a minute to be able to elevate himself to get on his friend's back. The most simple move to get a piggyback ride took all the strength he had. The other friend opened the door and they disappeared into the darkness. That good-looking young man will face the stares of people for the rest of his life wondering what is wrong with him. The simplest tasks he took for granted in his favorite sports will now only be a memory. His courage will have to last a lifetime.

Revival is sweeping Colorado's youth, and many are taking a bolder stand for their faith. This clearly has been the case in other schools too. I saw this in my school—a few miles from Columbine—just a couple weeks after the Columbine tragedy during a meeting with students who were trying to cope with a classmate's suicide. As they were sharing, one student, Angie, announced, "We need to pray. We need to pray right now!" We prayed, and then she said, "This is serious stuff, and some of you guys might get mad at me, but I'm going to say it anyway. We all need think about where we're going to go when we die—to heaven or hell. None of us know when our last day will be, and we just need to be prepared." I was jumping up and down inside and saying, "You go, girl!" to her silently. No one mocked Angie because she was a key part of that group.

The students of Columbine High School will be forever changed because of the tragedy on April 20, 1999. Their faith has impacted the world. We can learn from the courage of our youth.

Don't let anyone look down on you because you are young,
but set an example for the believers
in speech, in life, in love, in faith and in purity.

1 TIMOTHY 4:12

Sometimes You See the Face of God

WILL MCKEAND

t first I was hesitant to go on tour with my youth choir. I thought that we would sing for a bunch of churches and not have any fun at all—except for going to Six Flags Over Georgia and being with a lot of girls. At our first stop, however, I realized that I was completely off base about the whole trip.

Our first concert was held at the Skinner Center for Special Needs, a center for physically and mentally challenged children. Most of us were expecting a stuffy church filled mostly with adults who came because they felt they needed to. Instead, we found a room full of kids of all ages, jumping out of their seats just to get a look at us.

Our director had instructed some of us to sit with the kids while we sang. I was scared, not of what the kids would think, but of what my friends would think. I did not want to look stupid.

As soon as I sat down to sing with the kids, one little boy reached over, grabbed my hand, and smiled as he tried to sing the songs with me. At that moment, I did not care what my friends thought; I did not even know they were there. All I knew was that there were fifty-plus children in that room who were dying to reach out to us for attention and for love.

At the end of the song, I reached over and gave the boy a hug.

Immediately, all the other kids were reaching out for me to hug them too. So I did, and so did the rest of the choir.

After the concert, the children invited us to join them for a party. Soon all of us were dancing except for one boy who sat in a wheelchair over in the corner. I asked if he wanted to dance, but his disease prohibited him from responding. However, while keeping him company, I noticed him staring at everyone dancing and having fun. I figured maybe he did want to dance after all; so I got up, wheeled him out on the dance floor, and pushed him back and forth to the music. He immediately lit up like a light bulb, smiling and waving his arms around trying to dance. When the song was over, he looked up at me as if to say thank you.

When it was time to go, our youth minister began to thank the children for inviting us to the party. One girl ran up, took the microphone from him, and began to sing out the best she could, "I may be slower than you, I may not be as fast as you, but don't forget me.... God is not done with me yet, God is not done with me yet."

It was the most incredible thing anyone could ever experience. What a difference we all can make by doing the simplest of things! We touched those children; and they touched us, no matter how different we were from one another. Like that young girl, I hope God is not done with me yet. I want to make more people feel the way I did that day, for it was at that moment I realized the real purpose of our choir tour...and of my life.

A Sister's Example

CRAIG BOERSMA

growing up is hard to do. I cannot imagine how I could have gotten by without the love, support, and good example that my sister Cheryl has provided.

Cheryl's actions have always given me hope; her advice has always been sound; and her love for the Lord has only grown stronger over the years.

I remember driving in the car with her about four years ago. We were taking a friend home who was having a hard time in his life and was doing some things he shouldn't have been.

"Why do you do it?" she asked. "How can you keep doing this when you know how much it is hurting God?"

As she cried and prayed for him that night, I was amazed at Cheryl. I had never thought about it that way before and, even if I had, I doubt I would have had the courage to ask such questions.

This is just one of the major instances in which my sister's actions were a huge encouragement to me. She speaks her beliefs without hesitation, stands up for her convictions in all sorts of situations, and is filled with the most amazing joy I have ever seen in anyone. I wouldn't trade her for anything.

Your very lives are a letter that anyone can read by just looking at you.
Christ Himself wrote it—not with ink, but with God's living Spirit;
not chiseled into stone, but carved into human lives.

2 CORINTHIANS 3:2–3
THE MESSAGE

57 Cents

DR. RUSSELL H. CONWELL
FROM *ACRES OF DIAMONDS*

a sobbing little girl stood near a small church from which she had been turned away because it 'was too crowded.' "I can't go to Sunday school," she sobbed to the pastor as he walked by. Seeing her shabby, unkempt appearance, the pastor guessed the reason and taking her by the hand, took her inside and found a place for her in the Sunday school class. The child was so touched that she went to bed that night thinking of the children who have no place to worship Jesus.

Some two years later, this child lay dead in one of the poor tenement buildings and the parents called for the kindhearted pastor, who had befriended their daughter, to handle the final arrangements. As her poor little body was being moved, a worn and crumpled purse was found which seemed to have been rummaged from some trash dump. Inside was found 57 cents and a note scribbled in childish handwriting which read, "This is to help build the little church bigger so more children can go to Sunday school."

For two years she had saved for this offering of love. When the pastor tearfully read that note, he knew instantly what he would do.

Carrying this note and the cracked, red pocketbook to the pulpit, he told the story of her unselfish love and devotion. He challenged his deacons to get busy and raise enough money for the larger building. But the story does not end there!

A newspaper learned of the story and published it. It was read by a realtor who offered them a parcel of land worth many thousands. When told that the church could not pay so much, he offered it for a 57 cent payment.

Church members made large subscriptions. Checks came from far and wide. Within five years the little girl's gift had increased to $250,000.00—a huge sum for that time (near the turn of the century). Her unselfish love had paid large dividends.

When you are in the city of Philadelphia, look up Temple Baptist Church, with a seating capacity of 3,300, and Temple University, where hundreds of students are trained. Have a look, too, at the Good Samaritan Hospital and at a Sunday school building which houses hundreds of Sunday scholars, so that no child in the area will ever need to be left outside at Sunday school time.

In one of the rooms of this building may be seen the picture of the sweet face of the little girl whose 57 cents, so sacrificially saved, made such remarkable history.

inspiration

Music of the World

Kind words are the music of the world.
They have power that seems to be
beyond natural causes,
as if they were some angel's song
that had lost its way and come to earth.

FREDRICK WILLIAM FABER

Rich or Poor?

AUTHOR UNKNOWN

One day a father took his rich family and his son on a trip to the country with the firm purpose of showing him how poor people can be. They spent a day and a night on the farm of a very poor family. When they got back from their trip the father asked his son, "How was the trip?"

"Very good, Dad!"

"Did you see how poor people can be?" the father asked.

"Yeah!"

"And what did you learn?"

The son answered, "I saw that we have a dog at home, and they have four. We have a pool that reaches to the middle of the garden, they have a creek that has no end. We have imported lamps in the garden, they have the stars. Our patio reaches to the front yard, they have a whole horizon."

When the little boy was finished, his father was speechless.

His son added, "Thanks, Dad, for showing me how poor we are!"

A Guy Named Bill

REBECCA MANLEY PIPPERT
FROM *OUT OF THE SALTSHAKER*

his name is Bill. He has wild hair, wears a T-shirt with holes in it, jeans and no shoes. This was literally his wardrobe for his entire four years of college. He is brilliant. Kind of esoteric and very college. He became a Christian while attending college.

Across the street from the campus is a well-dressed, very conservative church. They want to develop a ministry to the students, but are not sure how to go about it.

One day Bill decides to go there. He walks in with no shoes, jeans, his T-shirt, and wild hair. The service has already started and so Bill starts down the aisle looking for a seat. The church is completely packed and he can't find a seat. By now people are looking a bit uncomfortable, but no one says anything.

Bill gets closer and closer and closer to the pulpit and when he realizes there are no seats, he just squats down right on the carpet. (Although perfectly acceptable behavior at a college fellowship, trust me, this had never happened in this church before!) By now the people are really uptight, and the tension in the air is thick.

About this time, the minister realizes that from way at the back of the church, a deacon is slowly making his way toward Bill. Now the deacon is in his eighties, has silver-gray hair, a three-piece suit, and a pocket watch. A godly man—very elegant, very dignified, very courtly. He walks with a cane and as he starts walking toward this boy, everyone is saying to themselves, *You can't blame him for what he's going to do. How can you expect a man of his age and of his background to understand some college kid on the floor?*

It takes a long time for the man to reach the boy. The church is utterly silent except for the clicking of the man's cane. All eyes are focused on him. You can't even hear anyone breathing. The people are thinking, *The minister can't even preach the sermon until the deacon does what he has to do.* And now they see this elderly man drop his cane on the floor. With great difficulty he lowers himself and sits down next to Bill and worships with him so he won't be alone. Everyone chokes up with emotion.

When the minister gains control he says, "What I'm about to preach, you will never remember. What you have just seen, you will never forget."

When Charlie Sings

SAUNA WINSOR

It's called a "sing thing." Maybe you've heard of them. Here in the great Northwest, they are very big. Hundreds, and sometimes thousands, of Christian teenagers cram themselves together in a church and sing praises to God. It's like popcorn. You come fairly excited to sing and fellowship with other students, and then, when it all begins, you cannot contain yourself. The Holy Spirit does not miss these occasions. Students come from hours away come for a chance to hear what heaven will sound like.

I remember my first time. I was always happy to find a fun place to hang out, and I love to sing. I had heard what to expect—lots of people, cool songs, and yes, guys. But, I had no idea that one boy would make an impact on me. Me—a confident, self-centered teen. An impact that, no doubt, I will remember for the rest of my life.

We sang about ten songs or so. They usually ran together and were very loud, then quiet, then loud again. There was so much excitement in the air. All these kids wanted to praise the Lord. It was fun to fit in.

After about forty minutes, I remember a youth pastor from one of the churches came to the front and talked. He was telling us what a privilege it was to worship God openly—without fear of going to jail or even worse, dying for being a Christian. He talked about how God loves to hear us sing to Him—how He loves to hear us praise His Name.

Then, the pastor told us he wanted to introduce us to a friend of his. His friend's name was Charlie. Charlie was born with a mental condition that caused his brain to function abnormally. Charlie loved Jesus. And he loved to sing to Him. When the youth pastor called Charlie up to the platform, some of the band members leading worship looked surprised. Then I noticed what they had noticed. Not only was Charlie tall and gangly and awkward, he just didn't look "normal." He was dressed like all the rest of us, but he was definitely not "normal."

The youth pastor continued. He said that Charlie's favorite song was "Jesus Loves Me," and Charlie wanted to sing it for us. I remember wondering what a person that looked like Charlie would sound like.

As the band began to play, I was overwhelmed with emotion. I couldn't tell if I was sad, guilty, thankful, or what. I watched as Charlie sang his heart out for his Savior. To us, his singing was terrible and hard to listen to for very long. If I hadn't recognized the tune, I would not have known he was singing "Jesus Loves Me." I watched and listened realizing Charlie believed every word he was singing. Yes, Jesus did love him. I wondered, *When God hears our praises, does He hear our voices or does He hear our hearts?* I don't know. But, one thing I do know—He loves it when Charlie sings.

Shout with joy to the Lord, Oh earth!
Worship the Lord with gladness.
Come before him, singing with joy.

Psalm 100:1–2
New Living Translation

Everything I Need for Joy

MAX LUCADO
FROM *THE APPLAUSE OF HEAVEN*

have everything I need for joy!" Robert Reed said.

"Amazing!" I thought.

His hands are twisted and his feet are useless. He can't bathe himself. He can't feed himself. He can't brush his teeth, comb his hair, or put on his underwear. His shirts are held together by strips of Velcro. His speech drags like a worn-out audio cassette.

Robert has cerebral palsy.

The disease keeps him from driving a car, riding a bike, and going for a walk. But it didn't keep him from graduating from high school or attending Abilene Christian University, from which he graduated with a degree in Latin. Having cerebral palsy didn't keep him from teaching at a St. Louis junior college or from venturing overseas on five mission trips.

And Robert's disease didn't prevent him from becoming a missionary in Portugal.

He moved to Lisbon, alone, in 1972. There he rented a hotel room and began studying Portuguese. He found a restaurant owner who would feed him after the rush hour and a tutor who would instruct him in the language.

Then he stationed himself daily in a park, where he distributed brochures about Christ. Within six years, he led seventy people to the Lord, one of whom became his wife, Rosa.

I heard Robert speak recently. I watched other men carry him in his wheelchair onto the platform. I watched them lay a Bible in his lap. I watched his stiff fingers force open the pages. And I watched people in the audience wipe away tears of admiration from their faces. Robert could have asked for sympathy or pity, but he did just the opposite. He held his bent hand up in the air and boasted, "I have everything I need for joy."

His shirts are held together by Velcro, but his life is held together by joy.

The joy of the Lord is your strength!

NEHEMIAH 8:10

Through a Father's Eyes

LONNI COLLINS PRATT

saw the car just before it hit me. I seemed to float. Then darkness smashed my senses.

I came to in an ambulance. Opening my eyes, I could see only shreds of light through my bandaged, swollen eyelids. I didn't know it then, but small particles of gravel and dirt were embedded in my freckled sixteen-year-old face. As I tried to touch it, someone tenderly pressed my arm down and whispered. "Lie still."

A wailing siren trailed distantly somewhere, and I slipped into unconsciousness. My last thoughts were a desperate prayer: "Dear God, not my face, please...."

Like many teenage girls, I found much of my identity in my appearance. Adolescence revolved around my outside image. Being pretty meant I had lots of dates and a wide circle of friends.

My father doted on me. He had four sons, but only one daughter. I remember one Sunday in particular. As we got out of the car at church, my brothers—a scruffy threesome in corduroy and cowlicks—ran ahead. Mom had stayed home with the sick baby.

I was gathering my small purse, church school papers, and Bible. Dad opened the door. I looked up at him, convinced in my seven-year-old heart that he was more handsome and smelled better than any daddy anywhere.

He extended his hand to me with a twinkle in his eye and said, "A hand, my lady?" Then he swept me up into his arms and told me how pretty I was. "No father has ever loved a little girl more than I love you," he said.

In my child's heart, which didn't really understand a father's love, I thought it was my pretty dress and face he loved.

A few weeks before the accident, I had won first place in a local pageant, making me the festival queen. Dad didn't say much. He just stood beside me with his arm over my shoulders, beaming with pride. Once more, I was his pretty little girl, and I basked in the warmth of his love and acceptance.

About this me time, I made a personal commitment to Christ. In the midst of student council, honor society, pageants, and parades, I was beginning a relationship with God.

In the hours immediately after my accident, I drifted in and out of consciousness. Whenever my mind cleared even slightly, I wondered about my face. I was bleeding internally and had a severe concussion, but it never occurred to me that my concern with appearance was disproportionate.

The next morning, although I couldn't open my eyes more than a slit, I asked the nurse for a mirror. "You just concern yourself with getting well, young lady," she said, not looking at my face as she took my blood pressure.

Her refusal to give me a mirror only fueled irrational determination. If she wouldn't give me a mirror, I reasoned, it must be worse than I imagined. My face felt tight and itchy. It burned sometimes and ached other times. I didn't touch it, though, because my doctor told me that might cause infection.

My parents also battled to keep mirrors away. As my body healed internally and strength returned, I became increasingly difficult.

At one point, for the fourth time in less than an hour, I pleaded for a mirror. Five days had passed since the accident.

Angry and beaten down, Dad snapped, "Don't ask again! I said no and that's it!"

I wish I could offer an excuse for what I said. I propped myself on my elbows, and through lips that could barely move, hissed, "You don't love me. Now that I'm not pretty anymore, you just don't love me!"

Dad looked as if someone had knocked the life out of him. He slumped into a chair and put his head in his hands. My mother walked over and put her hand on his shoulder as he tried to control his tears. I collapsed against the pillows.

I didn't ask my parents for a mirror again. Instead, I waited until someone from housekeeping was straightening my room the next morning.

My curtain was drawn as if I were taking a sponge bath. "Could you get me a mirror, please?" I asked. "I must have mislaid mine." After a little searching, she found one and discreetly handed it to me around the curtain.

Nothing could have prepared me for what I saw. An image that resembled a giant scraped knee, oozing and bright pink, looked out at me. My eyes and lips were crusted and swollen. Hardly a patch of skin, ear-to-ear, had escaped the trauma.

My father arrived a little later with magazines and homework tucked under his arm. He found me staring into the mirror. Prying my fingers one by one from the mirror, he said, "It isn't important. This doesn't change anything that matters. No one will love you less."

Finally he pulled the mirror away and tossed it into a chair. He sat on the edge of my bed, took me in his arms, and held me for a long time.

"I know what you think," he said.

"You couldn't," I mumbled, turning away and staring out the window.

"You're wrong," he said, ignoring my self-pity.

"This will not change anything," he repeated. He put his hand on my arm, running it over an IV line. "The people who love you have seen you at your worst, you know."

"Right, seen me with rollers or with cold cream—not with my face ripped off!"

"Let's talk about me then," he said. "I love you. Nothing will ever change that because it's you I love, not your outside. I've changed your diapers and watched your skin blister with chicken pox. I've wiped up your bloody noses and held your head while you threw up in the toilet. I've loved you when you weren't pretty."

He hesitated. "Yesterday you were ugly—not because of your skin, but because you behaved ugly. But I'm here today, and I'll be here tomorrow.

Fathers don't stop loving their children, no matter what life takes. You will be blessed if life only takes your face."

I turned to my father, feeling it was all words, the right words, spoken out of duty—polite lies.

"Look at me then, Daddy," I said. "Look at me and tell me you love me."

I will never forget what happened next. As he looked into my battered face, his eyes filled with tears. Slowly, he leaned toward me, and with his eyes open, he gently kissed my scabbed, oozing lips.

It was the kiss that tucked me in every night of my young life, the kiss that warmed each morning.

Many years have passed. All that remains of my accident is a tiny indentation just above one eyebrow. But my father's kiss, and what it taught me about love, will never leave my lips.

Along the Path

AUTHOR UNKNOWN

water bearer in India had two large pots, each hung on each end of a pole which he carried across his neck. One of the pots had a crack in it, and while the other pot was perfect and always delivered a full portion of water at the end of the long walk from the stream to the master's house, the cracked pot arrived only half full.

For a full two years, this went on daily, with the bearer delivering only one and a half pots full of water to his master's house. Of course, the perfect pot was proud of its accomplishments...perfect to the end for which it was made. But the poor, cracked pot was ashamed of its own imperfection, and miserable that it was able to accomplish only half of what it had been made to do.

After two years of what it perceived to be a bitter failure, it spoke to the water bearer one day by the stream. "I am ashamed of myself, and I want to apologize to you."

"Why?" asked the bearer. "What are you ashamed of?"

"I have been able, for these past two years, to deliver only half my load because this crack in my side causes water to leak out all the way back to your master's house. Because of my flaws, you have to do all of this work, and you don't get full value from your efforts," the pot said.

The water bearer felt sorry for the old, cracked pot, and in his compassion he said, "As we return to the master's house, I want you to notice the beautiful flowers along the path."

Indeed, as they went up the hill, the old, cracked pot took notice of the sun warming the beautiful wildflowers on the side of the path, and this cheered it some. But at the end of the trail, it still felt bad because it had leaked out half its load, and so again, the pot apologized to the bearer for its failure.

The bearer said to the pot, "Did you notice that there were flowers only on your side of the path, but not on the other pot's side? That's because I have always known about your flaw, and I took advantage of it. I planted flower seeds on your side of the path, and every day while we walk back from the stream, you've watered them. For two years I have been able to pick these beautiful flowers to decorate my master's table. Without you being just the way you are, he would not have had this beauty to grace his house."

Each of us has our own unique flaws. But if we will allow it, the Lord will use our flaws to grace His Father's table. In God's great economy, nothing goes to waste. Don't be afraid of your flaws. Acknowledge them, and you too can be the cause of beauty. Know that in our weakness we find our strength.

My gracious favor is all you need.
My power works best in your weakness.

2 CORINTHIANS 12:9A
NEW LIVING TRANSLATION

Giving and Keeping

JIM ELLIOT
WHO DIED A MARTYR FOR HIS FAITH

He is no fool

who gives what he cannot keep,

to keep what he cannot lose.

Graduation Speech

TIM WILDMON
RETOLD BY ALICE GRAY

They walked in tandem, each of the ninety-three students filing into the already crowded auditorium. With rich maroon gowns flowing and the traditional caps, they looked almost as grown up as they felt. Dads swallowed hard behind broad smiles, and moms freely brushed away tears.

This class would not pray during the commencement—not by choice but because of a recent court ruling that prohibited it. The principal and several students were careful to stay within the guidelines allowed by the ruling. They gave inspirational and challenging speeches, but no one mentioned divine guidance and no one asked for blessings on the graduates or their families. The speeches were nice, but they were fairly routine.

Until the final speech received a standing ovation.

A solitary student walked proudly to the microphone. He stood still and silent for just a moment, and then he delivered his speech—a resounding sneeze. The rest of the students rose immediately to their feet, and in unison they said, "God bless you."

The audience exploded in applause. This graduating class found a unique way to invoke God's blessings on their future—with or without the court's approval.

The Story of the Praying Hands

AUTHOR UNKNOWN

around 1490 two young friends, Albrecht Dürer and Franz Knigstein, were struggling young artists. Since both were poor, they worked to support themselves while they studied art.

Work took so much of their time and advancement was slow. Finally, they reached an agreement: They would draw lots, and one of them would work to support both of them while the other would study art. Albrecht won and began to study, while Franz worked at hard labor to support them. They agreed that when Albrecht was successful he would support Franz who would then study art.

Albrecht went off to the cities of Europe to study. As the world now knows, he had not only talent but genius. When he had attained success, he went back to keep his bargain with Franz. But Albrecht soon discovered the enormous price his friend had paid. For as Franz worked at hard manual labor to support his friend, his fingers had become stiff and twisted. His slender, sensitive hands had been ruined for life. He could no longer execute the delicate brush strokes necessary to fine painting. Though his artistic dreams could never be realized, he was not embittered but rather rejoiced in his friend's success.

One day Dürer came upon his friend unexpectedly and found him kneeling with his gnarled hands intertwined in prayer, quietly praying for the success of his friend although he himself could no longer be an artist. Albrecht Dürer, the great genius, hurriedly sketched the folded hands of his faithful friend and later completed a truly great masterpiece known as "The Praying Hands."

Today art galleries everywhere feature Albrecht Dürer's works, and this particular masterpiece tells an eloquent story of love, sacrifice, labor, and gratitude. It has reminded multitudes around the world of how they may also find comfort, courage, and strength.

"There is no situation so chaotic that God

cannot, from that situation, create

something that is surpassingly good.

He did it at the creation.

He did it at the cross.

He is doing it today."

BISHOP MOULE

Rocks to Inspire

STEPHEN COVEY

a high school science teacher wanted to demonstrate a concept to his students. He takes a large mouth jar and places several large rocks in it. He then asks the class, "Is it full?" Unanimously, the class replies, "Yes!"

The teacher then takes a bucket of gravel and pours it into the jar. The small rocks settle into the spaces between the big rocks. He then asks the class, "Is it full?" This time there are some students holding back but most reply, "Yes!"

The teacher then produces a large can of sand and proceeds to pour it into the jar. The sand fills up the spaces between the gravel. For the third time, the teacher asks, "Is it full?" Now most students are wary of answering, but again many reply, "Yes!"

Then the teacher brings out a pitcher of water and pours it into the jar. The water saturates the sand. At this point the teacher asks the class, "What is the point of this demonstration?"

One bright young student raises his hand and then responds, "No matter how full one's schedule is in life, he can always squeeze in more things!"

No," replies the teacher, "the point is that unless you first place the big rocks in the jar, you are never going to get them in. The big rocks are the important things in your life—your family, your friends, your personal growth. If you fill your life with small things—as demonstrated by the gravel, the sand, and the water—you will never have the time for the important things.

He will give you all you need from day to day if you live for
him and make the Kingdom of God your primary concern.

MATTHEW 6:33
NEW LIVING TRANSLATION

Third-String Nobody

RETOLD BY DUKE DUVALL

oach Lou Little was preparing his football team for the 1934 Rose Bowl when a third-string senior—a young man who had scarcely gotten off the bench the whole season—approached him with a request.

"Coach, I'm going to ask a big favor of you," he began.

"What is it, son?" Coach Little asked.

"I need to arrive at the Rose Bowl the day of the game," the young man answered.

Both coach and player realized this was a most unusual request since the rest of the team would arrive several days in advance to prepare for the biggest game of the year.

"Why do you need to do that?" Coach Little asked.

"My dad died a few days ago," the player said, "and I need to be home with my mom for a few days—but I'll be there in time for the game, for sure."

"Son, I'm sorry to hear about your dad," Coach Little replied. "Why don't you go home and stay with your mom instead of returning for the game?"

Knowing that there was little chance this four-year bench warmer would play in the Rose Bowl, Coach Little thought he was doing the young man a favor by releasing him. He truly believed it would be in the young man's best interest to stay at home, but the player would have none of it.

"Coach, you don't understand!" he protested. "I would never let you or the team down like that. I don't want to miss out on the game. I'm just asking if I can show up the day of the game."

Seeing the player's determination, Coach Little finally granted his request.

True to his word, on January first, the young man arrived at the Rose Bowl and went straight to the locker room and dressed for the game. He then tracked down the coach because he had one more request—a request most players in his position would never have the nerve to even think about.

"Coach," he began, looking Lou Little in the eye with all the earnestness he could muster, "you've got to let me start today. Please! I promise you, you won't be sorry."

Coach Little would later say, "I don't know what got into me. Even though the young man had never started a game in four years, I found myself agreeing to his request. I guess I figured that since we won the coin toss and since we were going to be receiving, I could put him into block and just take him out after the first play without any damage...."

What happened next, amazed everyone. The kick fell short, and the player designated to receive the kick didn't get it. Instead, the young man who was a third-string player was the one carrying the ball. Ignited with passion, he took off and made it all the way down to the twenty-yard line!

For some reason Coach Little decided to leave him in the game. The opening run was scored and play after play, it was this former third-string nobody who became the deciding factor in the stunning upset in the Rose Bowl that day. The young man was carried off the field by his teammates.

Later that evening, when the stands were empty except for the clean-up crew, Coach Little noticed a solitary figure standing alone out on the fifty-yard line. When he realized it was the young player, Coach Little approached him. "Son, you've been a part of this team for four years. You've been faithful in showing up for practice; you've always done whatever I have asked of you, but I've never seen the player that played here today. Today you played with passion. What made the difference?"

"Coach, have you ever seen my parents on campus?" he asked.

"As a matter of fact, I have. I never met them, but remember being impressed with how much in love they seemed to be. I always saw them arm in arm everywhere they went."

"Well, Coach, they were very much in love, but that's not the main reason you always saw them arm in arm. My father was blind. My mother helped guide him when he didn't want to use a white cane. For four years, my dad came to every home game, listening to the loudspeaker and hoping to hear the announcer mention my name. But that never happened—mostly because I never gave it my all. As you know, a few days ago my daddy died. And Coach, today was the first game that my daddy could see me play, and that made all the difference."

Let's never forget that our heavenly Father always sees us. He is there tenderly watching over us and cheering us on. It makes all the difference.

God...I'm an open book to you;
even from a distance, you know what I'm thinking.
You know when I leave and when I get back;
I'm never out of your sight.

PSALM 139:1–3
THE MESSAGE

Life 101

PHIL CALLAWAY
FROM *WHO PUT THE SKUNK IN THE TRUNK?*

I'm learning that some of the most successful people I know didn't have a clue what the future held on graduation day.

I'm learning that a good sense of humor is money in the bank. In life. On the job. In a marriage.

I'm learning that a good attitude can control situations you can't. That any bad experience can be a good one. It all depends on me.

I'm learning that you can do something in an instant, that will give you heartache for life.

I'm learning that bitterness and gossip accomplish nothing, but forgiveness and love accomplish everything.

I'm learning that it takes years to build trust, and seconds to destroy it.

I'm learning to always leave loved ones with loving words. It may be the last time I see them.

I'm learning that if I'm standing on the edge of a cliff, the best way forward is to back up. That you don't fail when you lose, you fail when you quit.

I'm learning that too many people spend a lifetime stealing time from those who love them the most. Trying to please the ones who care about them the least.

I'm learning that money is a lousy way of keeping score. That true success is not measured in cars, or homes, or bank accounts, but in relationships. Put God first. The others will follow.

I'm learning that having enough money isn't nearly as much fun as I thought it would be when I didn't have any. That money buys less that you think. A house but not a home. Vacations but not peace. Sex but not love.

I'm learning that helping others is far more rewarding than helping myself. That those who laugh more worry less. That when I grow up I wanna be a kid.

I'm learning that you cannot make anyone love you. But you can work on being loveable.

I'm learning that I will never regret a moment spent reading the Bible or praying. Or a kind word. Or a day at the beach.

I'm learning that laughter and tears are nothing to be ashamed of. To celebrate the good things. And pray about the bad.

And I'm learning that the most important thing in the world is loving God. That everything good comes from that.

"WHEN I COME TO THE SKATE PARK TO WITNESS,
I FIND IT BEST TO WEAR THE WHOLE PADDING OF GOD."

"EVER SINCE TOM BECAME A CHRISTIAN,
NO ONE HARASSES THE BIBLE CLUB ANYMORE."

"DON'T LOOK NOW, BUT HERE COMES THE FREAK."

"I WENT LAST YEAR TO CHANGE LIVES.
I CAME BACK WITH THE BIGGEST
CHANGE BEING MY OWN!"

"WIN OR LOSE GOD,
MAKE THIS OUR MISSION FIELD."

"LOOK AT IT THIS WAY... WE FAILED MR. SMITH'S TEST ON EVOLUTION, BUT WE PASSED GOD'S TEST OF FAITH!"

"WANNA RACE?"

trust and courage

My Shield and My Protector

The LORD is my rock, my fortress, and my savior;
my God is my rock, in whom I find protection.
He is my shield, the strength of my salvation, and my stronghold.

PSALM 18:2
NEW LIVING TRANSLATION

Courage Under Fire

PETER HENDERSON
AS TOLD TO SANDRA P. ALDRICH

I was in fifth period biology class, where my classmates and I were teasingly trying to talk our teacher, Mrs. Williams, out of giving us the week's quiz.

Suddenly, the floor began to shake, and we could hear what sounded like a stampede below our second-story classroom. My first thought was, *Boy, the seniors are getting a little out of hand with their annual prank!* But that idea was barely formed when sounds like firecrackers, followed by screams, reached us. Suddenly the business teacher from down the hall ran into our room.

"Everyone get down! They're shooting!" she shouted.

Those of us in the front dove under our desks. Mrs. Williams began to herd students into the greenhouse in the back, calling to the rest. It wasn't until she called my name that I scrambled from under my desk and joined the forty others squeezed into that tiny space, which was roughly six-by-fifteen feet. Several boys as well as the girls had begun to cry, so Mrs. Williams, appearing wonderfully calm, said, "Everything's going to be okay. Just sit down on the floor; stay away from the windows."

As I listened to the muffled sobs around me, I thought, *A fight must have started at lunch, and now somebody is shooting up the building. How can this be happening here, of all places? Columbine High School is one of the best in Colorado.*

One of the greenhouse doors faced the stairs, so as the shots got closer, we knew whoever was shooting was coming our way. Suddenly we could hear two guys shouting back and forth to each other in the hall.

I whispered, "Lord, what's going on? Please protect us." Immediately, I felt as though a protective blanket dropped over me, and while the situation was not okay, I knew we would be.

Then the guys just beyond our door began to scream profanities to each other. They had absolutely lost it emotionally. At times they didn't even sound human, as though they were directly under Satan's control. I'd never heard anything like that, and it gave me the weirdest feeling to hear their frenzied shouting.

All we could tell from the voices was that the gunmen were teens and that more than one were doing the shooting. They'd leave for a few minutes, fire off more rounds, then return to reload their guns. If they got separated, they yelled to each other. At times the walls shook as more bombs went off. At one point, one of the gunmen excitedly yelled, "Today I'm gonna die! Yeah!"

Inside the greenhouse, we huddled together, listening to the shots and screams coming from the library just down the hall. Suddenly the beeper of a boy near the window went off, startling us. Several students whispered, "Shhh!"

The boy quickly turned off the sound and glanced at the number. "It's my dad," he whispered apologetically. Then another beeper went off prompting more shushing. "My folks," the girl behind me said. Then yet another beeper.

"Take out the batteries," someone whispered hoarsely. "They'll give us away."

As batteries were being pulled out, we thought about our worried families. Whatever was going on, they had more information than we did. Then we could hear police sirens outside and could see through the back windows the police helicopters hovering over the school. Whatever was going on was bad.

For more than an hour, the crazed shouting, the shooting, the screams continued. Then an eerie silence descended. The forty of us huddled on the floor for three and a half hours, whispering prayers and whispering about our worried families.

Then new voices sounded down the hall. Startled, we looked toward the door. Then an adult male called, "Cover this section." We could hear heavy footsteps and an answering. "Ready!"

Suddenly the door was pulled open. Several students gasped, but standing before us was a black-uniformed SWAT team member. "It's okay; come on, stay behind the shields. Hurry!" he said.

We scrambled up from the floor and faced a line of SWAT team members holding shields on their left to protect us as we scurried, heads down, on their right. As we moved past the dining commons, we could see the chaos of shattered windows, books and lunch trays scattered about, and book bags tossed aside. *Boy, whoever did this was really angry,* I thought.

It wasn't until we were outside and turned the corner that we saw two bodies sprawled on the sidewalk near the school. *Wait. This wasn't just a lunchroom fight. What happened here?* I thought. Never in those long greenhouse hours had I imagined that those shots actually were *killing* people. "Come on, kids, come on. Head to the cars," the shield-bearing SWAT team member urged. We hurried past the bodies, concentrating on the police cars waiting at the end of the sidewalk. From the school, we were taken to nearby Clement Park, where we were questioned for several minutes. Later, as the police and Red Cross workers escorted us to school buses, reporters and TV cameramen hurried beside us, behind the yellow police barricades. "Where were you kids?" they shouted. "Were any of you in the room with the dying teacher?"

A dying teacher? My thoughts were tumbling together. We ignored the reporters and kept moving toward the waiting vehicles.

Safely on the bus, some of the students broke into tension-relieving sobs. Most of us were still in shock, too stunned to talk. From the two school counselors on the bus, we learned only that the gunmen had set off bombs and wounded several students. We were being taken to the nearby elementary school where our families were waiting.

As we arrived at the school, worried parents watched each of us enter through the stage area, hoping to see their son or daughter. From the platform, I saw my parents waiting with all of our church's ministers. I ran down the steps and fell into their embrace.

Throughout the long night that followed, the accounts came in of students who had not reported in, including my friend Cassie Bernall. The next day, we learned that the gunmen had shot themselves in the library, but not before killing twelve students and a teacher, Coach Sanders, and that twenty-three others had been wounded. At least three of the Christian kids—Cassie Bernall, Rachel Scott, and Valeen Schnurr—had been asked by the gunmen if they believed in God before being shot. All three had answered yes, but only Valeen survived.

I had been closest to Cassie since we'd had lunch together every day the previous semester, so I felt terrible when I heard she had died. But I wasn't surprised to learn she had declared her faith even with a gun pointed at her head. A few years ago she had been dabbling in Satanism, but had accepted the Lord and started leading a vivacious Christian life. She had seen what Satan had to offer, and she saw what God had to offer—and she chose God.

In the weeks that followed, more information came as we tried putting our lives back together and attending classes at a neighboring high school. But it wasn't until the last day of school that the teacher who had been across the hall from the Greenhouse Club, as we now call ourselves, told us that as he barricaded his door with desks, he saw the gunmen dash into our classroom. When they found it empty, they ran down the hall. If the forty of us hadn't been in the greenhouse, the murders very well could have started in our biology lab.

I'm often asked how God could let this happen. But as evil as this situation is, I remind myself that 500 people were supposed to die, according to the gunmen's plans. After all, there were a thousand students in the dining commons when the kitchen bomb was set to go off, and that device alone would have killed several hundred if the timer hadn't malfunctioned. I see that "failure" as God's direct intervention. God is still in charge. And He will continue to bring His good out of it.

This tragedy is a prime example of the Genesis 50:20 principle of Joseph telling his brothers that what they meant for evil, God meant for good. One of the things I trust will come out of this evil is the three-part plan I helped develop through our Bible club, called "The Columbine Call to Action." Within a few days of the tragedy, our Bible club met and agreed we have to let other Christians know they are not powerless, and as they reach out to others, good things happen. After all, our Bible club had started with three and had grown to eighty—not bad for a public high school—so we knew God had provided us with an audience.

At that meeting, I suggested that Christian students do the following three things:

1. Pray for their schools and their classmates.
2. Get to know someone who is different from you.
3. Start a Bible club in their school or, if they already have one, become active in it.

God has been preparing us for this time. He took the evil plot that Satan hatched, and He is using it for His good. I find refuge in the truth of 1 John 4:4 that the One who is in us is greater than the one who is in the world. But I also feel a sense of urgency that if this evil is going to stop, we Christians must be the ones to reach out boldly and present Jesus to a hurting world. If we do, evil will not prevail, and the enemy will not win.

Don't let evil get the best of you,
but conquer evil by doing good.

ROMANS 12:21
NEW LIVING TRANSLATION

Our Refuge

PSALM 46:1–3
NEW LIVING TRANSLATION

God is our refuge and strength,
always ready to help in times of trouble.
So we will not fear,
even if earthquakes come
and the mountains crumble into the sea.
Let the oceans roar and foam.
Let the mountains tremble as the waters surge!

The Rich Family

EDDIE OGAN

'll never forget Easter 1946. I was fourteen, my little sister Ocy twelve, and my older sister Darlene sixteen. We lived at home with our mother, and the four of us knew what it was to do without many things.

My dad had died five years before, leaving Mom with seven school-age kids to raise and no money. By 1946 my older sisters were married and my brothers had left home.

A month before Easter, the pastor of our church announced that a special Easter offering would be taken to help a poor family. He asked everyone to save and give sacrificially.

When we got home, we talked about what we could do. We decided to buy fifty pounds of potatoes and live on them for a month. This would allow us to save $20 of our grocery money for the offering.

Then we thought that if we kept our electric lights turned out as much as possible and didn't listen to the radio, we'd save money on that month's electric bill. Darlene got as many house and yard cleaning jobs as possible, and both of us baby-sat for everyone we could. For fifteen cents, we could buy enough cotton loops to make three pot holders to sell for $1. We made $20 on pot holders.

That month was one of the best of our lives. Every day we counted the money to see how much we had saved. At night we'd sit in the dark and talk about how the poor family was going to enjoy having the money the church would give them. We had about eighty people in church, so we figured that whatever amount of money we had to give, the offering would surely be twenty times that much. After all, every Sunday the pastor had reminded everyone to save for the sacrificial offering.

The day before Easter, Ocy and I walked to the grocery store and got the manager to give us three crisp $20 bills and one $10 bill for all our change. We ran all the way home to show Mom and Darlene. We had never had so much money before. That night we were so excited we could hardly sleep. We didn't care that we wouldn't have new clothes for Easter; we had $70 for the sacrificial offering. We could hardly wait to go to church!

On Sunday morning, rain was pouring down. We didn't own an umbrella, and the church was over a mile from our home, but it didn't seem to matter how wet we got. Darlene had cardboard in her shoes to fill the holes. The cardboard came apart and her feet got wet. But we sat in church proudly. I heard some teenagers talking about the Smith girls having on their old dresses. I looked at them in their new clothes, and I felt so rich.

When the sacrificial offering was taken, we were sitting in the second row from the front. Mom put in the $10 bill, and each of us girls put in a $20. As we walked home after church, we sang all the way. At lunch Mom had a surprise for us. She had bought a dozen eggs, and we had boiled Easter eggs with our fried potatoes!

Late that afternoon the minister drove up in his car. Mom went to the door, talked with him for a moment, and then came back with an envelope in her hand. We asked what it was, but she didn't say a word. She opened the envelope, and out fell a bunch of money. There were three crisp $20 bills, one $10 and seventeen $1 bills.

Mom put the money back in the envelope. We didn't talk, we just sat and stared at the floor. We'd gone from feeling like millionaires to feeling like poor white trash.

We kids had had such a happy life that we felt sorry for anyone who didn't have parents like ours and a house full of brothers and sisters and other kids visiting constantly.

We thought it was fun to share silverware and see whether we got the fork or the spoon that night. We had two knives, which we passed around to whoever needed them.

I knew we didn't have a lot of things that other people had but I had never thought we were poor. That Easter Day I found out we were. The minister had brought us the money for the poor family, so we must be poor.

I didn't like being poor. I looked at my dress and worn-out shoes and felt so ashamed that I didn't want to go back to church. Everyone there probably already knew we were poor! I thought about school. I was in the ninth grade and at the top of my class of over 100 students. I wondered if the kids at school knew we were poor. I decided I could quit school since I had finished the eighth grade. That was all the law required at that time.

We sat in silence for a long time. Then it got dark, and we went to bed. All that week, we girls went to school and came home, and no one talked much. Finally on Saturday, Mom asked us what we wanted to do with the money. What did poor people do with money? We didn't know. We'd never known we were poor.

We didn't want to go to church on Sunday, but Mom said we had to. Although it was a sunny day, we didn't talk on the way. Mom started to sing, but no one joined in, and she only sang one verse.

At church we had a missionary speaker. He talked about how churches in Africa made buildings out of sun-dried bricks, but they needed money to buy roofs. He said $100 would put a roof on a church. The minister said, "Can't we all sacrifice to help these poor people?"

We looked at each other and smiled for the first time in a week. Mom reached in her purse and pulled out the envelope. She passed it to Darlene, Darlene gave it to me, and I handed it to Ocy. Ocy put it in the offering.

When the offering was counted, the minister announced that it was a little over $100. The missionary was excited. He hadn't expected such a large offering from our small church. He said, "You must have some rich people in this church."

Suddenly, it struck us! We had given $87 of that "little over $100." We were the rich family at the church! Hadn't the missionary said so?

The Victor's Crown

RETOLD BY ALICE GRAY

During his reign as emperor of Rome, Nero had powerful young wrestlers who competed on his behalf. Every day during their long, arduous workouts and before each tournament, they would chant in unison, "We wrestle for thee alone, O Nero, to win for thee the crown." Among these mighty athletes was Vespasian—a brilliant leader—outstanding in strength and loyalty.

One winter a message was sent to Nero advising him that forty of his wrestlers had become Christians, and they were no longer dedicating their power and strength to Nero, but instead to Christ. Nero summoned Vespasian and told him that all forty of the wrestlers were to be killed if they did not renounce their loyalty to Christ. However, rather than kill them outright, the wrestlers were to be stripped naked and sent out in the bitter cold to spend the night on a frozen lake until they either froze to death or renounced their faith.

A group of Roman soldiers built a campfire close to the shore and huddled around the warmth as they guarded the freezing wrestlers. Vespasian joined the soldiers in their vigil. Throughout the frigid night, the wrestlers called out in unison; "We forty wrestle for Thee alone, O Christ, to win for Thee the crown." During the darkest hours when the temperature dropped the lowest, their voices became weaker and weaker but still they called out, "We forty wrestle for Thee alone, O Christ, to win for Thee the crown."

Shortly before dawn, one wrestler lost courage and stumbled toward the soldiers and warmth of the fire. Rather than freeze to death, he would relent. At the edge of the lake you could still hear the faint voices of the other wrestlers, "We thirty-nine wrestle for Thee alone, O Christ..."

As Vespasian heard their pledge, he stripped himself and walked out on the frozen lake to where the others stood. As the sun rose the soldiers heard Vespasian's strong voice mingled with the others, "We forty wrestle for Thee alone, O Christ."

If we die with him,
we will also live with him.

2 TIMOTHY 2:11
NEW LIVING TRANSLATION

Byron

LYNN DIXON

It was one of those mornings when our homeroom teacher couldn't be there. She had a meeting or a doctor appointment and would be coming later. Whenever this happened our homeroom class would be held in a room at the back of the library. This way, we were somewhat supervised. That is to say that as long as we didn't make a huge ruckus, we could pretty much do as we pleased. This was typically not a problem. After all we were seniors and didn't need someone hovering over us to make us behave.

Homeroom classmates are usually an interesting mix. Our homeroom class had a mix of the popular cheerleader types, the jocks, the brains, the party crowd, the ordinary kind of "fall between the cracks" kids—and then there was the Satanist. I was, to my knowledge, the only professing Christian in the group. It was in this setting that it happened.

Eva, who was a pretty, new girl in school, started crying. Of course, several of us showed concern. She told us that Byron, the Satanist, had threatened her with a hex. He had told her that she was going to die. At this I couldn't keep quiet.

"Eva, if you know and trust Christ as your Savior then there is nothing that Byron can do to you. God, not Byron, holds your life in His hands." At this point, I had everyone's attention in the room, especially Byron's. He was not thrilled at my challenging his powers. From this point on, he turned his threats towards me.

A typical homeroom morning would go something like this: I would go in and sit down; we had our moment of silence; and if I didn't have any homework to do, I would pull out my Bible and start to read. Pretty soon I could expect Byron to start in. Sometimes he would make direct threats to me from behind my back. Oh, did I mention that his assigned seat was right behind mine? Most of the time, he would discuss what he and his Satanist friends were going to do to me. When he became bored with trying to intimi-date me, he would try to gross me out with vulgar descriptions of movies he had seen or of homosexual activities. My response to Byron was always simple and brief.

"Byron, God loves you and I'm praying for you. I'm not scared of you because God holds my life in His hands."

Most of the time, I didn't give Byron's muttered threats a second thought, but every now and then I would wonder if he might try to act out his threats. During those times I prayed for guidance and protection. Ultimately, I would come to the same conclusion. I concluded that if the worst did happen and Byron killed me, I would rather die in Christ than to live without Him.

I made it through that homeroom period that year by praying regularly for Byron, and God did an amazing thing. He actually gave me a love and compassion for Byron. I began to see through his ugly, vulgar facade and saw an empty, searching, and hurting soul. Jesus tells us in Matthew 5:44-45: "But I tell you: Love your enemies and pray for those who persecute you, that you may be sons of your Father in heaven."

The last time that I saw Byron was at my high school graduation. He came up to me and for the final time said, "I'm going to kill you." I looked up at him and for the final time replied, "God loves you and I'll be praying for you."

It has been a long time since I was a senior in high school, but occasionally I think of Byron. When I think of him, I still pray that if he doesn't already know Christ's incredible, all-encompassing love—that he will know it soon.

The Man in Charge

BETTY AND RAY WHIPPS
AS TOLD TO SUSAN WALES
FROM *A MATCH MADE IN HEAVEN, VOLUME II*

a s a young man I had big plans for my life. The war was raging in Europe, and, wanting to serve my country, I enlisted in the Navy Air Corp. As a young cadet, with dreams of flying military aircraft, I found the competition among the men was fierce. When the grades were posted, I was relieved to discover that I had made a high B, until a mentoring officer pulled me aside and gave me a dose of reality.

"Ray, you're a good soldier," he said, "but there's so much competition in the navy that you most likely won't make the cut with a B." Sensing my disappointment, the officer suggested, "Why don't you go back home and apply for Army Air Corp? You'd make an excellent pilot, and there's not as much competition in that branch. They'll be lucky to get you."

Those words were music to my ears. With renewed hope, I headed back home. Fortunately, I knew the lady who ran the draft board in my hometown of Columbus, Ohio. After I explained my situation, she promised me that she would put a hold on my papers until the next crop of recruits was admitted into the Army Air Corp. It would only delay my plans for a matter of weeks. I was flying high on hope.

I was shocked a few days later when I went to the mailbox and found the letter with the news: I was about to be drafted into the army. My entry into the Army Air Corp was only days away. *How could this have happened?* I wondered. I figured a trip down to the draft board was all I needed to straighten this mess out. I found out that while my friend at the draft board was away on vacation another woman in the office had processed my papers. Now there was nothing that could be done. I was drafted.

My hopes and dreams of becoming a pilot were permanently dashed when I was assigned to the Infantry Division of the United States Army. "Why Lord?" I questioned. Despair flooded my being. And yet I was strengthened knowing that God had a plan for me. Maybe it wasn't the plan I had in mind, but I knew without a doubt that I had to trust Him. My family rallied around me lending their support and prayers.

After basic training, I was shipped off to Europe just after D-Day. I arrived on French soil and was immediately placed on the front lines, where we faced combat every day. Through all that, my faith in God sustained me. I prayed often and kept the New Testament the Army had issued me in my pocket, close to my heart, often seeking it for words of comfort and faith.

My days on the front line were filled with the horrors of war. Death was all around me. Each time I watched the American planes overhead from my foxhole, my heart broke a little more. I wondered if God realized I was supposed to be up there and not down here on the front line. *Did God forget me?* I wondered.

Our division was assigned to General Patton and we fought through Normandy and the Saint Lo breakthrough. During the siege, my hands were wounded with shrapnel and I was taken away to have them bandaged. This injury probably saved my life, because when I returned to the outfit; I was horrified to discover that only three men—including me—were left in my platoon.

From Saint Lo we marched into Paris and liberated the city. It was obvious to me that God had intervened to spare my life. I was then assigned to another platoon. Next we headed for the Hurtegn Forest in Germany. We dug foxholes and put covers over them because artillery shells were hitting the tree-tops and crashing down on us. Again, as I looked up at the planes fighting in the sky above me, I cried out, "Lord, don't You know that I'm supposed to be up there and not down here? Why didn't You give me my dream of flying?"

I went on out to check on my men, when suddenly an 80 shell, a weapon used by the Germans, came close and barreled me over. I felt a sting. The shrapnel had gone through the front of my right thigh. I was treated in the field by my platoon sergeant. As he walked me back to the aid station, I had to step over the dead soldiers lying in the forest. I was thankful to be alive.

The medics transported me to a hospital in Belgium for surgery, but before I could undergo the procedure, the hospital was bombed. My fate again was suddenly changed when all the patients had to be transported to Paris, where we were scheduled on a flight to England. When we arrived in Paris, a thick, heavy fog hung over the airport and our plane couldn't take off.

Once again, I found out how God had intervened. While we waited for a train to the hospital in Cherbourg, France, I saw one of the fellows from my platoon and asked, "How did we do on our attack of the village?"

"There's nobody left but you and me, Sarge," he told me.

Our entire platoon was wiped out. I was awestruck that God had spared me.

The first morning I awoke in the Cherbourg hospital, an attractive Army nurse with a beautiful smile and a pen and paper in her hand greeted me with a smile. I rubbed my eyes, wondering if she was a figment of my imagination. But then she spoke.

"Write to your wife," she instructed me, "and tell her you're alive and safe and sound in a hospital in France."

"I don't have a wife," I confessed.

"Well, write to your girlfriend, then," she prodded.

There was a girl back home, but I quickly forgot her as I gazed into the beautiful hazel eyes of the nurse before me. I was sure I wasn't the first soldier to look wistfully into those eyes, but I wanted to be the last. The nurse, whose name I learned was Betty, was very professional and a bit standoffish. But she was simply obeying orders. All the nurses had been warned not to fraternize with enlisted men. Their major had sternly warned them, "You'll be sent to the hospital in the Philippines." While the pretty nurse's mannerisms said no, her eyes told me that she had an interest in me. I was not about to give up easily.

Betty and I became better acquainted each day as she nursed me back to health. One day when she appeared she noticed that I was reading my New Testament. We were both delighted to discover that we shared the Christian faith, and we began talking about the Lord. I relayed to her how God had miraculously spared me time and time again in the battlefield. Our Christian fellowship strengthened our relationship, and I then knew without a doubt that God had orchestrated all those circumstances to bring me to this place to meet this special woman.

The hospital at Cherbourg was only allowed to keep a patient for thirty days, and as I watched the pages on the calendar change each day, I knew I had to work quickly to win the pretty nurse's heart. I was being sent to England to recuperate and would be sent back to battle as soon as I regained my strength.

When the time came for me to go to Oxford to recuperate, I was saddened to tell Betty good-bye. I presented her with a gold wedding band that I had found on the battlefield, and she promised to wear it around her neck on a dog tag chain in remembrance of me. I managed to get a promise from her that she would write to me in Oxford.

Our letters crossed the English Channel with speed and regularity. We were becoming better acquainted through the mail. With each letter we were falling more and more deeply in love.

I knew what I felt for this woman, and I knew it was real. But it was going to take a miracle of God to keep us together.

When I recovered from my injury, I was sent back into the battlefield in Germany. One night when we were advancing, I became disoriented and separated from my group. Because of the shadows in the German forest, I thought the trees were my men. I suddenly found myself in a small German village. Praying all the while that God would protect me, I finally made my way to a home of a farmer about three miles behind our line. I'll never forget the look on his face when an American soldier appeared at his door. In broken German I tried to explain to the farmer and his terrified family that I was there in peace, that I was lost and exhausted and needed a place to sleep. Eventually, the farmer led me to his barn where I prayed for a safe night of sleep. It was not to be.

I was later awakened by a group of German soldiers the farmer had led to me. I was terrified as I cradled my New Testament close to my heart. *There will be no more letters to Betty now,* I thought.

The Germans didn't know quite what to do with me, so I traveled with them. All the time I was with them, American forces were attacking them—

and me—from all sides. *How ironic!* I thought. *I'll be killed by my own men.*
When we reached the POW camp in Munich, they handed me over as an
escaped prisoner. When I embraced the other prisoners, both French and
American, they took care of some minor wounds I had incurred along the
way. That night, the camp was bombed so we had to be transported to the
dreaded Stalag VII A in Munich.

I was aware that Munich was one of the targets that American forces had
planned to bomb, so I expressed some concern for our lives.

"What are you worried about?" a fellow prisoner asked. "You're listed as
an escaped prisoner. You're scheduled to be shot at dawn with a group of us."

"Were these the plans You had for me all along, Lord?" I prayed. Is this
how my life is going to end?

With the stark realization that I was about to meet my Maker, my
thoughts traveled to home, family, and Betty, the pretty nurse who, unbe-
knownst to her, I'd planned to make my wife. I knew I would never see her
again. I spent the night on my knees praying and seeking solace from my
battered New Testament. I prayed that God would somehow intervene in
this hopeless situation. The men surrounding me were encouraged to have
a Christian among them. I was their ray of hope.

Back in France, Betty had been devastated when one of her letters to me
was returned marked "killed in action." At that moment she realized just how
much she loved me. She was numb with grief as she went through the motions
of caring for her patients. The news of losing me was more than she could bear.

But Betty's spirits soared when the next morning another letter arrived
marked missing in action. Hope flooded her as she prayed every moment for
my safety. She was very much in love with me, as I was with her.

Perhaps it was Betty's prayers that night, but the Americans chose on the
eve of my death watch to bomb Munich. Amid the rubble and confusion I
was spared, and in a matter of days American soldiers marching through
Munich liberated us. The war was over.

I was sent to France to recover and then sent home. When I returned
home my mother received a letter from Betty asking if she had heard from
me. I answered the letter myself but somehow it had the wrong APO (post
office) box. But as Betty was leaving for home, someone ran up to her and

handed her my letter just as she boarded the ship. She has since said she was surprised that I hadn't heard her scream all the way to America.

Betty and I were reunited back in the States, where we finished out our duties after brief furloughs. We finally rendezvoused in New Orleans, where I was stationed. That is where we became man and wife.

The bride didn't wear a white gown but her uniform. I also wore mine. We were proud to wear our military dress, and it was also our tribute to the armed forces, which God used to bring us together.

As I look back over my wartime service, I realized that God was in charge all along. Without God's divine appointment, my path would never have crossed with Betty's. If I hadn't been wounded, I would have never met her.

God had led me into the battles through the long and winding path that led me to the woman He had for me. My disappointments were transformed into joy through these difficult circumstances. I am still in awe at how God had His hand on me and carried out His plans for my life through some bitter disappointments.

He had a plan all along. Little did I realize when I was so devastated over not realizing my dream of flying that God had something better in store for me.

Since the day I left the service, the Lord has been in charge of my life. I have learned to remember that when the going gets rough during the courses of our lives, He still has a plan.

He is the man in charge!

Trust God from the bottom of your heart;
don't try to figure out everything on your own.
Listen for God's voice in everything you do,
everywhere you go; he's the one who will keep you on track.

PROVERBS 3:5–6
THE MESSAGE

Emergency Phone Numbers

When in sorrow . . . . call John 14

When men fail you . . . . call Psalm 27

If you want to be fruitful . . . . call John 15

When you have sinned . . . . call Psalm 51

When you worry . . . . call Matthew 6:19–34

When you are in danger . . . . call Psalm 91

When God seems far away . . . . call Psalm 139

When your faith needs stirring . . . . call Hebrews 11

When you are lonely and fearful . . . . call Psalm 23

When you grow bitter and critical . . . . call 1 Corinthians 13

For Paul's secret to happiness . . . . call Colossians 3:12–17

For ideas of Christianity . . . . call 1 Corinthians 5:15–19

When you feel down and out . . . . call Roman 8:31–39

When you want peace and rest . . . . call Matthew 11:25–30

When the world seems bigger than God . . . . call Psalm 90

When you want Christian assurance . . . . call Romans 8:1–30

When you leave home for labor or travel . . . . call Psalm 121

When your prayers grow selfish and narrow . . . . call Psalm 67

For a great opportunity . . . . call Isaiah 55

When you want courage for a task . . . . call Joshua 1

How to get along with fellow men . . . . call Romans 12

When you think of investments . . . . call Mark 10:17–31

If you are depressed . . . . call Psalm 27

If your pocketbook is empty . . . . call Psalm 37

If you lose confidence in people . . . . call 1 Corinthians 13

If people seem unkind . . . . call John 15:12–17

If discouraged about your work . . . . call Psalm 126

If you find the world growing small and yourself great . . . . call Psalm 19

Emergency numbers may be dialed direct.

No operator assistance necessary.

All lines are open to Heaven 24 hours a day!

Feed your faith, and doubt will starve to death!

Straight A's

HELEN HEAVIRLAND

What would Jesus do?

I asked myself the question. But I didn't like the answer.

I'd wanted desperately to get straight A's this quarter. I'd studied hard from the beginning. Now it was test week, and I had a major test each day. I planned an intense review the night before each and felt confident of the coveted straight A's until...until the Denneys telephoned.

Mr. and Mrs. Denney begged me to go to a rock and gem exhibition on Thursday evening. The Denneys were an elderly couple who had been very kind to me. But I didn't want to go. Especially not any evening this week. Definitely not Thursday. The biology exam was Friday morning, and biology was my hardest subject. If I went to the rock and gem show, there'd be no time left for review. But when I asked "What would Jesus do?" I sensed that He would go. Dreams of straight A's collapsed into a nightmare.

Each evening—until Thursday—I reviewed the subject for the next day's final. Thursday evening I went to the rock and gem show. On my way home a small voice whispered, *You could review biology rather than spend your evening quiet time with God.*

Another voice reminded me, "Seek ye first the kingdom of God, and his righteousness..." (Matthew 6:33).

A battle raged. "God wouldn't mind..."

"Seek ye first..."

"Just this once?"

"Seek ye first..."

On my knees after Bible study I pleaded, "Please, God, don't let me worry. I really wanted an A. I've studied hard all quarter. I planned to review this evening. But I did what I thought You wanted me to do. Please help me do well on my test tomorrow, if that's Your will."

I fell asleep quickly.

When the alarm jangled me awake, I immediately remembered a dream I'd had during the night. In the dream I sat in the biology classroom. The teacher stood and said, "Put your books away. Get out your paper and pencils. It's time for the biology test." Books swished shut and thudded into desks. Papers shuffled. Then silence. The teacher continued, "I'm going to do something different today. I'm going to write your test on the board."

That certainly is different, I thought in the dream. *He never writes our tests on the blackboard.* He strode to the board and wrote, filling the wide blackboard with four rows of questions. And now that I was awake I still saw each question clearly, as if it were etched in my mind.

Again that morning, I was tempted to review biology rather than spend my usual quiet time with God. "Seek ye first..., seek ye first...," conscience encouraged. I chose time with God.

The only time left for review was on the twenty-minute ride to school. *Where do I start?* I wondered.

There were a few questions on the test in my dream that I don't know the answers to, I thought. I might as well start there.

I looked up those answers, finding the last one just as we arrived at school.

When biology class began, the teacher stood and said, "Put your books away. Get out your paper and pencils. It's time for the biology test." His tone and inflections sounded strangely familiar. Books swished shut and thudded into desks. Papers shuffled. Then silence. The teacher continued, "I'm going to do something different today. I'm going to write your test on the board."

Chills raced down my spine as he strode to the blackboard and began writing. Question number one on the board was the same as in the dream! The second question was identical too. And the rest. Each question on the board—wording, spacing, punctuation, every detail—was a perfect replica of the test in the dream!

I got 100 percent on that test. But I received something far greater than straight A's. I felt overwhelmed by God's care for me. But I'd only glimpsed His care and power.

A little later the teacher mentioned, "I've been so busy lately that I didn't get to write the biology exam until after I got to school this morning."

My eyes popped open wide. "When did you get to school?" I asked.

"Eight-thirty," he answered matter-of-factly.

The chills raced down my spine again. I'd wakened before 7:00.

Faith out of Flames

CHERYL BOERSMA

I never dreamed that one single cloud of smoke in the sky could have such an impact on me. Maybe it was its shape that threatened my heart so strongly, or perhaps the fact that it was multiplying in size by the second. As it climbed higher into the sky, my fears soared with it. Little did I know that this cloud was the beginning of a lesson from God that I will never forget.

I spotted the gray cloud on my way home from school one spring day. Looking intently at the billowing smoke, I prayed that our worries were in vain, but when I saw the scene of shiny, red trucks and bright flashing lights ahead of us, my hopes shattered. The road near my house was completely blocked off by emergency vehicles and policemen. As I was trying to absorb this nightmare scene, the bus driver received the message that there was an out of control forest fire and it was headed for nearby homes. Every house in the area had been evacuated and we were instructed to return to school to meet our parents.

As the bus retreated back to school, I questioned God and demanded answers. *Why is this happening to me? Is my family safe? And what about my dog and cat?* A hard lump formed in my throat. I did not want to cry, but when I tried comforting those around me, a tear escaped and silently rolled down my cheek.

We filed off the bus and were greeted by open arms of friends and family. Camera teams and news crews were scattered around the area. Piles of cots were propped up against the walls, and tables were being set up for dinner as people scurried around getting things ready for the night.

To my relief, I found out that my family and pets were safe. Over the next few days, we all stayed at my uncle and aunt's house. From this safe distance, we huddled outside and watched the fire burn. Huge airplanes roared overhead carrying water and fire retardant. Every once in a while, a blast from the ground sent up black smoke with red flames whirling around and through it. I wondered if our house was safe and prayed that my worries would not come true.

During those days of uncertainty, I found that God was teaching me some lessons. First, I came to realize that I had been holding my earthly possessions too close to my heart, and God taught me to place value on things with eternal worth. He asked me to put my complete faith in Him, trusting that He is always in control and would never forget or forsake me. God also reminded me that He has a perfect plan, and even if my house did burn down, He had a reason for it

We were overjoyed when the news came that the fire was contained and we were allowed to return to our neighborhood. On the way back home, I was shocked to see that seven houses and many acres of trees had been destroyed. An area that was once dominated by mighty pines was now a forest of charred toothpicks. The sight of a simple, brown house, though, brought a smile back to my face. Our house had survived.

The time of the fire was tough, but the lessons were strong and life changing. Now whenever there is a cloud of smoke in the sky or when I see the barren area of land that has been ravaged by fire, I am reminded to put my complete faith in God, always.

You will keep in perfect peace all who trust in you, whose thoughts are fixed on you.

ISAIAH 26:3
NEW LIVING TRANSLATION

Spinning out of Control

SUSAN SMART

It was a beautiful Saturday morning, and I couldn't wait to get up in the air. I'd always wanted to fly. And now, just a few months after graduating from high school, my dream was coming true. I was taking flying lessons, and this particular day looked especially promising.

I was looking at the plane I'd be flying, a Cessna-150, when someone called my name.

"Hi Sue," said Jim, my flight instructor. "Ready for your third solo flight?"

"Yeah, I think so," I said, hesitating. Flying without Jim still felt weird, but as a student pilot, sooner or later I had to let go of my insecurity.

"Now remember," Jim said, "I want you to work on your stalls today. And don't be afraid to really stall the bird, Sue. You tend to recover too early, but I want to see you practice those stalls more thoroughly."

Jim was right: Stalls were not my best maneuver. They left me feeling shaky, so I tended to recover much sooner than necessary.

Learning stalls is a critical part of any flight training plan. A stall happens when the plane's air speed drops too low to keep flying. When done correctly, stalls are an important part of every safe landing. Pilots routinely practice their stalls at 5,000 feet or higher, where there is plenty of room to recover safely.

A few minutes later, I was airborne, and asking God for His protection. Even though this was only my third solo, Jim's quiet confidence in my ability encouraged me. Still I missed his reassurance from the other seat.

I was on my own.

At 5,000 feet, high above a small farming community, I looked down at the beautiful view. Taking several deep breaths to relax, I remembered Jim's words of instruction before practicing my stalls.

OK, I thought, *it's time to work.*

I started with a take-off stall, slowly but steadily pulling the nose back, keeping an eye on the airspeed: 65 knots...60...55...53...The warning buzzer began to squeal, so I quickly recovered, dipping the nose down while carefully easing back on the throttle.

You pulled out too quickly, I thought.

I remembered Jim's advice to "really stall the bird." So I set up for another one.

Jim, I thought, *I'm really going to stall it this time.*

With my left hand, I pulled back on the stick, propelling the plane upward. My right hand grasped the throttle, gradually reducing the engine's power.

"Everything's under control," I said to myself.

As the air speed began to drop, the stall-warning buzzer went off as usual, it's whine filling the tiny cockpit. Normally, I would recover at the earliest annoying sound of that buzzer, my skittish emotions compelling me to jump the gun. But not this time. No, I decided to let that buzzer screech as loudly as I could stand before pulling out of the stall.

I waited too long.

A slight, dropping lurch from the propeller was my only warning. Almost instantly, the left wing dipped, then tipped over, pitching the Cessna into a wing-over-wing spin.

Jerking my head around, I glanced out my side window. Instead of seeing the horizon, I gaped in horror at the ground. As the altimeter quickened its pace, unwinding at an alarming rate, headlines raced through my mind: "Student Pilot Killed in Spin."

Precious seconds grew incredibly long as I desperately tried to regain control over the little airplane. My frantic efforts only plunged it—and me—into an ever-tightening death spiral.

As I yanked and fought against the inevitable pull of gravity, words of wisdom somehow popped into my brain. A few weeks back, Jim had said, "If you ever get into a spin in a Cessna-150, just let go of the controls. It's built to fly on its own." Jim's words now reached into my confused thoughts, much like a life preserver thrown out to a drowning child. But could I trust them?

"Let go!" I screamed three or four times. My hands seemed glued to the controls. I was unable to pry my fingers off. Pulling hard one last time, I threw my arms up in the air, releasing my stranglehold on the yoke. I covered my face, bracing for impact.

Yawing and pitching wildly to the right, then to the left, the Cessna made grotesquely odd noises, something like the droning of a lawn mower that suddenly stops and then roars to life again. The shaking, shuddering gyrations gradually stilled. Amazingly, the airplane slowly but faithfully returned to straight-and-level flight. My eyes scanned the instrument panel, resting on the altimeter: 2,100 feet above sea level.

I had fallen more than half a mile. Jim was sitting at the front desk when I got back. I told him what had happened. And I told him I never wanted to fly again.

His blue eyes twinkling, Jim peered out the window toward the Cessna, now safely tied down.

"The plane looks fine to me, and you do too," he said, smiling. "You obviously remembered my advice. It worked, didn't it?"

I learned an important lesson that day: When I find myself in situations seemingly spinning out of control, God reminds me to let go of the controls of my life and trust Him.

He'll always return me to a straight-and-level course.

That's a promise...from on high.

God, you're my refuge. I trust in you and I'm safe!

PSALM 91:2
THE MESSAGE

Mandy's Ministry

EVA MARIE EVERSON

Last year, I was asked to teach a three-week class on Etiquette for Young Christian Men and Women. As I stood before the twenty or so men and women, I thought I was there to effect their young lives with my "knowledge" on etiquette.

Never could I have guessed the impact that one of them would have on me.

After the first class I was stopped in the foyer of the building by a beautiful, large-eyed girl of nineteen, Mandy Bradshaw. I knew of Mandy. Her parents and I had met at a Super Bowl party a few months previously, and I had heard her sing at a church production a few years earlier. However, that was all I knew.

"May I ask you a question?" Mandy asked in a voice that can only be described as vivacious.

"Certainly!" I said.

"Okay...when you are at a formal dinner party..." the questioning began. We stood dead center in the cacophony of young voices, as they chattered and laughed around us, discussing the art of fine dining. As we spoke, Mandy twisted a small band of white gold on her left ring finger.

"Are you married, Mandy?" I asked, noting the ring with my eyes.

"Oh, no!" she laughed easily, then extended her hand. "See? This band is engraved True Love Waits. That's how I feel. I'm not ashamed to stand here and tell you that I'm a virgin and I plan to stay that way until I get married! I wear this as a testimony to others and a reminder to myself. I've made a commitment to God that I never plan to break!"

"Good for you!" I exclaimed. "You are certainly a rare and special treat, Mandy Bradshaw!"

A few months later Mandy joined the worship team of our church. Each week as she stepped out onto the stage and behind the music stand she looked down at me (sitting in my regular front row seat) and winked. I'd wink back. It was an unspoken language we shared: Our hearts seemed to be bonded in a way I couldn't explain.

I heard a lot about Mandy as the days and weeks continued. Mandy had a personal ministry of drawing people together—making strangers feel welcomed, the unloved feel loved, and the hopeless feel hopeful. Whenever I was at the church, I saw her sprinting here and there, her eyes wide and her mouth spread in a smile and a conversation. How could anyone not love Mandy?

On August third, as Mandy and her friend Erika were on their way to an evening church service, a man driving in the opposite direction suffered a seizure, crossed over several lanes of traffic, and hit Mandy broadside. The car was crushed by the impact and spun around to finally rest heading in the opposite direction. Traffic came to a halt. As only God could orchestrate, within the cars of the now backed-up traffic was a paramedic and a nurse, both carrying medical items that would prove necessary.

Erika was safely removed from the car, but getting Mandy out would take skill. Time was of the essence: An artery in Mandy's arm was severed, her teeth were clenched (a sign of head injury), and she appeared to be losing the battle of life and death.

As the paramedic and nurse removed Mandy from the car, people began to step out of their cars and into the August heat. They stood in huddled masses and began to offer up prayers to God, asking for divine intervention while the paramedic performed an emergency tracheotomy and the nurse applied a tourniquet to Mandy's severed arm. A short while later, Mandy was airlifted to Orlando Regional Medical Center.

I received the call within hours. "So many people from church have gathered at the hospital," the caller reported. "Everyone is praying! Could you put out the word in your Internet prayer group, too?"

My Internet prayer group consisted of several hundred prayer warriors from all over the world. "Of course!" I said. "And if you see Rick and Pam tell them I'll see them tomorrow."

Over the course of the next three weeks, Mandy lingered in a coma in the Intensive Care Unit.

"I've never seen this many visitors for one patient...never heard this many people pray...." said the hospital's liaison to the media.

During their appearance (and win) on Destination Stardom, Mandy's friends Amy and Emily Pratt said to the entire world, "We sang this evening for a very special person, Mandy Bradshaw! We love you, girl!" Mandy was famous!

Over the next twenty-two weeks Mandy miraculously survived pneumonia, staph infection, and major surgery to remove a piece of IV tubing that had snapped loose and lodged in her heart. All the while, as she lay helpless in the cupped hands of God, the faith of all who love her grew from mustard seeds to mountains!

Last night I sat in Mandy's living room, a cozy room now dominated by a hospital bed, medical paraphernalia, and a special wheelchair that supports Mandy's head. Her large eyes looked at me with recognition, revealing a thousand things inside, though she is still unable to articulate what lies inside her heart. From a medical perspective, I know that Mandy shouldn't have survived the accident. From a spiritual perspective, I know that Mandy's ministry has continued in ways we can scarcely comprehend. Mandy proves every day that God is still in the healing business as she continues to bring people together through the voices of collective prayer. Even automobiles in the Central Florida area are subject to Mandy's ministry as they carry small flyers with her photograph and the words *Pray For Mandy!*

Later in the evening, in the quiet of my living room, I am privileged to hold the journals signed by well-wishers during those first few days after Mandy's accident. As I turn the pages, I am struck by the number of people who called Mandy "sweetheart." Each page records another testimony of how she touched their lives.

"We are all pulling for you every minute of every day," her friend Beth wrote. "You have made such a difference in my life!"

Cory wrote, "Know how much God is working in this whole situation. You have hundreds of people who are pullin' for you. Just remember how much God has done! He is awesome!"

Joane added, "You have sparked so much love and happiness all around you!"

Finally, in a tribute that truly exemplifies Mandy's ministry, Jay wrote: "Jesus has so much planned for you. You have already touched lives uncountable and will continue to be lifted up to the Lord. Healing will come and God is faithful and His love endures forever!"

I don't know why God allowed me the privilege of knowing Mandy, but every day I am so thankful, not only for her life, but also for being a part of a ministry that could not be stopped by tragedy. It only served to make it stronger.

The LORD your God is in your midst,

The Mighty One, will save;

He will rejoice over you with gladness,

He will quiet you with His love,

He will rejoice over you with singing.

ZEPHANIAH 3:17
NEW KING JAMES VERSION

changed lives

Scars

Faith Is…
Realizing that I am useful to God
not IN SPITE of my scars
but BECAUSE of them.

PAMELA REEVE

A Special Kind of Love

JOSH MCDOWELL
FROM *MORE THAN A CARPENTER*

I had a lot of hatred in my life. It wasn't something outwardly manifested, but there was a kind of inward grinding. I was (disgusted) with people, with things, with issues. Like so many other people, I was insecure. Every time I met someone different from me, he became a threat to me.

But I hated one man more than anyone else in the world. My father. I hated his guts. To me he was the town alcoholic. If you're from a small town and one of your parents is an alcoholic, you know what I'm talking about. Everybody knows. My friends would come to high school and make jokes about my father being downtown. They didn't think it bothered me. I was like other people, laughing on the outside, but let me tell you, I was crying on the inside. I'd go out in the barn and see my mother beaten so badly she couldn't get up, lying in the manure behind the cows. When we had friends over, I would take my father out, tie him up in the barn, and park the car up around the silo. We would tell our friends he'd had to go somewhere. I don't think anyone could have hated anyone more than I hated my father.

After I made my decision for Christ—maybe five months later—a love from God through Jesus Christ entered my life and was so strong it took that hatred and turned it upside down. I was able to look my father squarely in the eyes and say, "Dad, I love you." And I really meant it. After some of the things I'd done, that shook him up.

When I transferred to a private university I was in a serious car accident. My neck in traction, I was taken home. I'll never forget my father coming into my room. He asked me, "Son, how can you love a father like me?" I said, "Dad, six months ago I despised you." Then I shared with him my conclusion about Jesus Christ: "Dad, I let Christ come into my life. I can't explain it completely but as a result of that relationship I've found the capacity to love and accept not only you, but other people just the way they are."

Forty-five minutes later, one of the greatest thrills of my life occurred. Somebody in my own family, someone who knew me so well I couldn't pull the wool over his eyes, said to me, "Son, if God can do in my life what I've seen Him do in yours, then I want to give Him the opportunity." Right there my father prayed with me and trusted Christ.

Jesus was born into the family of men
that we might be born again into the family of God.

AUTHOR UNKNOWN

The Real Cassie

MISTY BERNALL
FROM *SHE SAID YES*

Three years ago in December, I quit my job to spend more time with my kids. My 13-year-old son Chris's grades were slipping at school. But it was 15-year-old Cassie who concerned me even more. She seemed to be growing increasingly distant by the day.

One day at home alone I remembered that my brother and his wife had given her a teen Bible, with a study guide giving young readers insights into dealing with their parents. Hoping to gain some tips myself, I wandered into Cassie's room and began looking through her drawers for it.

I found it all right, but I also found a stack of letters from her friend Mona (not her real name). My husband, Brad, and I had been concerned about Cassie's friendship with Mona ever since the fifth or sixth grade.

One day I had picked up Cassie with some of her girlfriends and thought how strange it was that when Mona got into the car, she folded her arms and put her head down. She seemed to be giving me a hostile signal that I was an impediment to her relationship with Cassie, and that she hated me for it.

Some instinct now overrode my usual respect for my daughter's privacy, and I began reading the letters. What I found in them froze me in my tracks.

The unprintable sex talk and profanity were bad enough. So were the references to the "fun" of contraband alcohol, marijuana and self-mutilation, and the adventures of a classmate whose girlfriend went to "this satanic church cult thing where you have to drink a kitten's blood to get in." The letters were decorated with knives, axes, and vampire teeth.

But what shocked me to my core was that several letters advised Cassie to do away with us and thus solve her innumerable problems. "Kill your parents!" one said. "Murder is the answer to all your problems." There were grisly drawings of a couple ("Ma and Pa") strung up by their intestines, daggers hanging from their hearts, of a crudely drawn knife dripping with "parent's guts" and of head stones for "Pa and Ma Bernall."

Dazed, I picked up the phone and called Brad. He came home, and we sat in stunned silence reading one letter after the next.

It seemed clear to us both that this was not a problem we could deal with alone. Over the next few hours we contacted Mona's mother, the sheriff's department and George Kirsten, our pastor at West Bowles Community Church. We copied a set of the letters for Mona's parents and a set for ourselves. The originals were filed with the sheriff. Then we sat and waited for Cassie.

When she breezed in from school we stopped her and told her what we'd found. At first she tried to play it down. "Oh, we didn't mean anything bad." Then, once she realized we were not about to let her off the hook, she flew into a screaming rage, accusing us of trampling on her rights by going through her bedroom without her permission.

This was a question that we would have to return to over and over in the months after that initial confrontation. Did we, as Cassie and later Mona and her mother claimed, "blow the whole thing way out of proportion"? Did we overstep the bounds of reasonable parenting by ignoring Cassie's "right to privacy"?

I can only say that I was afraid for my life. Brad never took the death threats as seriously as I did, but both of us felt we were dealing with something more than a bunch of rebellious teenagers. Unfashionable as it may be to suggest, I felt that we were engaged in a spiritual battle.

When we met with Mona's parents and a detective and investigator from the juvenile-crimes division, the police officers took the situation as seriously as we did and supported our desire for a restraining order to bar Mona from further contact with Cassie. The sheriff told Mona's parents that the letters were the worst he had seen during more than a decade in juvenile crime, and that if Mona had had any sort of prior record, she would have been called before a judge. Her parents showed no surprise or remorse, only hostility toward us.

In the following months, our struggle with Cassie developed into all-out war. She claimed we were holding her prisoner in her own home. But as Brad summed it up to her, she was to have "no freedom, no rights, no privileges, no trust. You're going to have to start right back at square one and earn all those things back."

We took her out of the public high school where Mona and other "friends" had gone and enrolled her and Chris in a private Christian school. The school is small and well-regulated, so we knew there was little chance Cassie would be able to escape the campus.

After school and on weekends we had to monitor her every step. We realized that we could demand sacrifices not only of Cassie; we also had to make sacrifices ourselves. Although we loved our house, we decided to move. Some of Cassie's old friends kept harassing us with hang-up telephone calls and drive-by taunts and peltings of our house with soda cans and eggs. We knew it was making her separation from them more difficult.

We also tried to regain Cassie's trust by working on our relationship—by holding our tongues when we were tempted to snap back at her, by trying to encourage her rather than nag, by offering her positive incentives rather than putting her under pressure or making sarcastic remarks.

I realized I had been trying to please Cassie and make her like me. I began to see my role as a parent in a new way—as a mentor and confidante, rather than a buddy.

All these efforts gradually began to have an effect. To my surprise, Cassie began to accept the boundaries I set for her. She even seemed *grateful* for them.

One day in spring 1997, about three months after Cassie had transferred to the Christian school, she came home and told us that a new school friend, Jamie, had invited her to a weekend youth retreat. In the hope that something good would come of it, we decided to let her go.

When we went to pick her up on Sunday, Brad and I were nervous to see Cassie arrive at the church with a bunch of girls who locked exactly like the type we had been trying to get her away from. But she came straight over to me, hugged me, then looked me in the eye and said, "Mom, I've changed. I know you are not going to believe it, but I'll prove it to you."

She never talked much about that weekend, and we never pressed her. Later we learned from her friend Jamie that after a nighttime worship service, Cassie had begun crying and pouring out her heart, asking God for forgiveness. In that weekend she reclaimed her soul.

From then on our daughter became a totally different person. Her eyes were bright, she smiled as she hadn't for years, and she began to treat us and her brother with genuine respect and affection. Now her life had a purpose beyond fighting back. Now there was hope.

At the end of summer 1997, between Cassie's freshman and sophomore years, Brad and I allowed her to transfer to Columbine High School, where she had a good friend. She developed new interests: photography, nature, poetry, Shakespeare.

She also began reading books that helped in her search for life's meaning. After her death Brad and I read through some of these, with their Hi-Liter markings and earnest handwritten notes. One sentence, from I. Heinrich Arnold's *Discipleship,* especially struck me: "All of us should live life so as to be able to face eternity at any time." I believe that in her last two years Cassie really did try to live that way, right up until April 20, 1999. On that date, confronted in the library of Columbine High by two young gunmen who asked her if she believed in God, Cassie said, "Yes"— and faced eternity.

In one of his first Sunday services after the death of my daughter, 13 of her schoolmates and one teacher in the shooting rampage, our assistant pastor, Dave McPherson, said, "The world looks at Cassie's 'yes' of April 20, but we need to look at the 'yes' she said day after day and month after month, before giving that final answer.

If I've learned anything from Cassie's short life, it is that no adolescent, however rebellious, is doomed by fate. I am sure that there must be a way to reach even the most alienated, hostile teen before it is too late. With warmth, self-sacrifice and honesty, with the love that ultimately comes from God—every child can be guided and saved. At least I will never give up that hope.

Love never gives up, never loses faith, is always hopeful,
and endures through every circumstance.

1 CORINTHIANS 13:7
NEW LIVING TRANSLATION

A Future and a Hope

JEREMIAH 29:11–13

"For I know the plans I have for you," declares the LORD,
"plans to prosper you and not to harm you,
plans to give you hope and a future.
Then you will call upon me and come and pray to me,
and I will listen to you. You will seek me and find me
when you seek me with all your heart."

Tommy

JOHN POWELL

ohn Powell, a professor at Loyola in Chicago, writes about a student in his Theology of Faith class named Tommy:

Some twelve years ago, I stood watching my university students file into the classroom for our first session in the Theology of Faith. That was the day I first saw Tommy. My eyes and my mind both blinked. He was combing his long flaxen hair, which hung six inches below his shoulders. It was the first time I had ever seen a boy with hair that long. I guess it was just coming into fashion then. I know in my mind that it isn't what's on your head but what's in it that counts; but on that day I was unprepared and my emotions flipped. I immediately filed Tommy under "S" for strange...very strange.

Tommy turned out to be the "atheist in residence" in my Theology of Faith course. He constantly objected to, smirked at, or whined about the possibility of an unconditionally loving Father/God. We lived with each other in relative peace for one semester, although I admit he was for me at times a serious pain in the back pew.

When he came up at the end of the course to turn in his final exam, he asked in a slightly cynical tone, "Do you think I'll ever find God?" I decided instantly on a little shock therapy. "No!" I said very emphatically.

"Oh," he responded, "I thought that was the product you were pushing." I let him get five steps from the classroom door and then called out, "Tommy! I don't think you'll ever find Him, but I am absolutely certain that He will find you!"

He shrugged a little and left my class and my life. I felt slightly disappointed at the thought that he had missed my clever line, "He will find you!" At least I thought it was clever.

Later I heard that Tommy had graduated and I was duly grateful. Then a sad report. I heard that Tommy had terminal cancer. Before I could search him out, he came to see me. When he walked into my office, his body was very badly wasted, and the long hair had all fallen out as a result of chemotherapy. But his eyes were bright and his voice was firm, for the first time, I believe.

"Tommy, I've thought about you so often. I hear you are sick." I blurted out.

"Oh, yes, very sick. I have cancer in both lungs. It's a matter of weeks."

"Can you talk about it, Tom?" I asked.

"Sure, what would you like to know?" he replied.

"What's it like to be only twenty-four and dying?"

"Well, it could be worse."

"Like what?"

"Well, like being fifty and having no values or ideals, like being fifty and thinking that booze, seducing women, and making money are the real 'biggies' in life."

I began to look through my mental file cabinet under "S" where I had filed Tommy as strange. (It seems as though everybody I try to reject by classification, God sends back into my life to educate me.)

"But what I really came to see you about," Tom said, "is something you said to me on the last day of class." (He remembered!)

He continued, "I asked you if you thought I would ever find God and you said, 'No!' which surprised me. Then you said, 'But He will find you.' I thought about that a lot, even though my search for God was hardly intense at that time. (My "clever" line. He thought about that a lot!) But when the doctors removed a lump from my groin and told me that it was malignant, then I got serious about locating God. And when the malignancy spread into my vital organs, I really began banging bloody fists against the bronze doors of heaven. But God did not come out. In fact, nothing happened. Did you ever try anything for a long time with great effort and with no success? You get psychologically glutted, fed up with trying. And then you quit.

"Well, one day I woke up, and instead of throwing a few more futile appeals over that high brick wall to a God who may be or may not be there, I just quit. I decided that I didn't really care…about God, about an afterlife, or anything like that. I decided to spend what time I had left doing something more profitable. I thought about you and your class and I remembered something else you had said: 'The essential sadness is to go through life without loving. But it would be almost equally sad to go through life and leave this world without ever telling those you loved that you had loved them.' So, I began with the hardest one, my dad. He was reading the newspaper when I approached him."

"Dad…"

"Yes, what?" he asked without lowering the newspaper.

"Dad, I would like to talk with you."

"Well, talk."

"I mean…it's really important."

The newspaper came down three slow inches. "What is it?"

"Dad, I love you. I just wanted you to know that."

Tom smiled at me and said with obvious satisfaction, as though he felt a warm and secret joy flowing inside of him, "The newspaper fluttered to the floor.

"Then my father did two things I could never remember him ever doing before. He cried and he hugged me. And we talked all night, even though he had to go to work the next morning. It felt so good to be close to my father, to see his tears, to feel his hug, to hear him say that he loved me. It was easier with my mother and little brother. They cried with me, too, and we hugged each other, and started saying real nice things to each other. We shared the things we had been keeping secret for so many years. I was only sorry about one thing: that I had waited so long.

"Here I was, just beginning to open up to all the people I had actually been close to. Then, one day I turned around and God was there. He didn't come to me when I pleaded with Him. I guess I was like an animal trainer holding out a hoop, 'C'mon, jump through.' 'C'mon, I'll give you three days, three weeks.' Apparently God does things in His own way and at His own hour. But the important thing is that He was there. He found me. You were right. He found me even after I stopped looking for Him."

"Tommy," I practically gasped, "I think you are saying something very important and much more universal than you realize. To me, at least, you are saying that the surest way to find God is not to make Him a private possession, a problem solver, or an instant consolation in time of need, but rather by opening to love."

"You know, the Apostle John said that. He said: 'God is love, and anyone who lives in love is living with God and God is living in him.' Tom, could I ask you a favor? You know, when I had you in class you were a real pain. But (laughingly) you can make it all up to me now. Would you come into my present Theology of Faith course and tell them what you have just told me? If I told them the same thing it wouldn't be half as effective as if you were to tell them."

"Oooh…I was ready for you, but I don't know if I'm ready for your class."

"Tom, think about it. If and when you are ready, give me a call." In a few days Tommy called, said he was ready for the class, that he wanted to do that for God and for me. So we scheduled a date. However, he never made it. He had another appointment, far more important than the one with me and my class. Of course, his life was not really ended by his death, only changed. He made the great step from faith into vision. He found a life far more beautiful than the eye of man has ever seen or the ear of man has ever heard or the mind of man has ever imagined.

Before he died, we talked one last time.

"I'm not going to make it to your class," he said.

"I know, Tom."

"Will you tell them for me? Will you…tell the whole world for me?"

"I will, Tom. I'll tell them. I'll do my best."

So, to all of you who have been kind enough to hear this simple statement about love, thank you for listening. And to you, Tommy, somewhere in the sunlit, verdant hills of heaven: "I told them, Tommy…as best I could."

Never Hopeless

When you say a situation
or a person is hopeless,
you are slamming the door
in the face of God.

REVEREND CHARLES ALLEN

Awash with Angels

KATHERINE G. BOND

O
utside the open window
The morning air is all awash with angels."

"This line," Mara pressed her finger against the warm overhead projector. "What do you think the poet Richard Wilbur is saying?"

The Junior Lit class squinted, as if she'd interrupted their collective nap. *Why do I even bother?* Mara thought wearily. *These kids don't care diddly about literature.*

She remembered the zeal of her early teaching; when she'd come barreling into class, singing her favorite poems until the kids caught the rhythm and picked up their pens. But now, Mara was tired. All the fire had gone out of it.

The bell rang and the kids hit the door like buckshot. "Don't forget the vocab test," she called after them.

Mara sank into her chair. Teaching had lost its flavor. Everything had—work, friendships, church had all begun to taste like unsalted potatoes. *Guess I'm not 25 anymore,* she thought.

But it wasn't that and she knew it. The truth was, since Dan walked out the door, Mara had lost faith in everything.

She flipped through some papers and then looked up. Natalie Moore was standing at the window. Her dark hair contrasted with her Goth makeup. How long had she been there, staring into the alley, without Mara noticing?

"Natalie?"

"It's clothes, isn't it?"

"What?"

Natalie pointed at clotheslines strung between aging apartment buildings. "Richard Wilbur's angels. He's talking about clothes hanging out, not about angels." Three earrings chimed faintly on her left ear.

"Well, it's…it's a metaphor."

"Oh." Natalie touched the anthology on Mara's desk. "Can I take it home?"

"The whole book?" Mara was surprised.

Natalie had spent her sophomore year slouched in the back row. Mara had removed headphones from her so many times she'd finally confiscated her CD player.

But now that Mara thought about it, she realized Natalie was different this year. A little less angry. Perhaps she'd grown up over the summer.

"You're welcome to the book," Mara told her. "In fact, I've got another copy. Why don't you keep it?"

"Really? Are you sure?"

"Take it," said Mara. *It seems so long since I've had anything to give.*

Natalie tucked the book inside her binder. "Thanks." She stood at the desk for a moment. Mara looked at her questioningly. "I…um, better run," the girl said, finally, and ducked out the door.

It stayed with her most of the afternoon—the spark in Natalie's eyes, the shy way she had taken the book. This was why Mara had gone into teaching. She was grateful to Natalie, though to admit it would seem unprofessional. Mara was there to teach students, not the other way around.

At home, she zapped a Budget Gourmet in the microwave and opened her plan book even though she had no planning left to do. It kept her from thinking too much. She and Dan had never had children. Mara knew she should be glad for that now, but she hated the empty house.

It would be nice to *be* a kid again, she thought—to have that blind trust she'd once had. It used to feel so safe at church when she was little, watching her arms turn multicolored in the light from the stained glass windows—as if she was a picture Jesus was painting.

Now church services seemed like just so many words to her. Mara didn't know why she bothered going.

But there was something she still longed for, something that kept eluding. Childishly, Mara wished for a world awash with angels.

Natalie was waiting when Mara arrived at school.

"I left my calculator," she mumbled. "Gotta have it for first."

Mara unlocked the door, secretly pleased to see her. "I'm making a pot of coffee," she offered. "Maybe you could use some."

"Sure, okay." Natalie shuffled in, smelling of soap. The calculator was on the sill. Natalie stopped to look out the window and watch the shirts, billowing like flags. "Thanks again for the book, Ms. Lee."

Mara poured. "I didn't know you liked poetry."

Natalie took the cup. "It's interesting, the way you teach it."

"I taught the same way all last year. It never interested you then."

Natalie stepped away from the desk. "Last year was last year," she said. "Aren't I allowed to be different now?"

Mara kicked herself. When had she begun to strike out, even at her students? Natalie picked up a cleaning rag and began rubbing the empty chalkboard, giving Mara sidelong looks. This kid was getting to her.

"Be different," Mara sighed. "Make your mark. That's what poets do. Just don't be afraid to stand alone."

"There are worse things than being alone." Natalie rubbed harder.

"Oh?" Mara swallowed, and the coffee went down hot and bitter.

"Yeah," said Natalie. "You know what's worse? When you wake up Saturday morning and don't know whose house you're at; when you find out your party friends don't really care about you, just whether you're cool enough to hang with—that's worse."

Mara put Natalie's cup in her hands. "That would be worse," she agreed. "Forgive me for sounding cynical."

"It's okay. I have a different kind of friends now." Natalie sat. She swirled the coffee. "You seem sad this year, Ms. Lee," she said finally. "I've noticed it, and other kids have too. We've—a bunch of us—have been praying for you."

Mara took a breath and ran her finger down the spine of her planbook. "Praying...for me?" She regretted that it came out so vulnerable, so like a plea.

Natalie shifted her boots on the tiles. "I know you're thinking I'm not a Jesus kind of kid," she said. "I didn't figure I was, either." She looked up. "But I couldn't get away from Him. He...loved me, even though..."

Even though...Mara looked at her hands; at the white line still visible on her third finger.

Natalie went on, gaining courage. "I don't know what you believe, Ms. Lee. I don't want to sound narrow-minded. But Jesus is the only one who will never leave you."

Mara stood, her hands on her planbook as Natalie gently set her cup down. "Thank you," she managed, as the girl walked out the door.

Mara pushed back from the desk, awakened by something bigger than the island-self she had become. It was Jesus, sweeter than she remembered. Jesus, who had never left.

Outside the window the brick walls faced off across the alley. Between them the lines laced back and forth, hung with fluttering white like Christmas decorations.

"Outside the open window
The morning air is all awash with angels."

She took a breath; leaned her head against the cool glass. "Oh God," she sobbed, "Oh, God!"

He heals the brokenhearted, binding up their wounds.

PSALM 147:3
NEW LIVING TRANSLATION

The True Definition of Success

JASON PROCOPIO
FROM *GROUP MAGAZINE*

Our youth group offers a special discipleship group called STORM (Student Training Outreach Ministry). My schedule was too busy for such an intensive program, but I attended the "graduation" for those who'd completed it.

My dad, who doubles as my youth pastor, invited STORM members up to a makeshift podium to share about the experience. Most of them gave glowing reviews. They talked about how God helped them get through the program, how much they learned, and how they were better Christians because of it.

Then it was Lucas' turn.

Lucas is one of my best friends. He makes people laugh everywhere he goes. He stumbled over his words. And then he burst into tears.

He cried for almost two minutes, then tried to get himself together. Through sobs, he said, "I was trying to decide whether I would come up here tonight, because I thought I might cry. Well, I'm cryin'." I heard a few scattered laughs.

"I didn't come here to say how proud I am and how thankful I am to everyone for helping me get through it—mainly because I didn't really get through it. I am here tonight to apologize. I wanted to apologize to Rob (a youth leader at our church who wrote STORM) for not taking his curriculum at full value. I think I came up here tonight more out of guilt than any-thing else. Because if you asked me what we learned in this program, I doubt I could tell you. I didn't learn half of what everyone else learned. I'm a slacker. I know it, you know it." A few more worried laughs as Lucas sat down.

My dad encouraged him a bit, told him he was being too hard on him-self. Then he tried to shift gears: "Well, now I…"

"Wait a minute, Glenn. I need to say something," Lucas' dad, Butch, politely interrupted my dad. He was standing. All eyes turned to him.

"For those of you who know Lucas and me, you know he's a lot like me. Some of you may feel sorry for him, but…but Lucas expresses his feelings better than I do." His chin began to quiver, and his bottom lip tucked in. Tears welled up in his eyes as he turned to his son.

"Lucas, you think that you failed at this. Well, let me be the first to tell you that you're not a failure." He looked at the rest of us. "When a teenager is in his room with the door shut, his parents can't help but worry. But I don't worry anymore. Because now I knock on his door and find him *praying* or read-ing his Bible. It's kind of strange when your teenage son comes to your bedroom and asks you if you've read your Bible today. But Lucas does. He's impacted me when I should've impacted him. And he got serious about it because of his desire to do well at STORM. You're not a failure, son. And I love you."

I couldn't help it anymore, I was bawling. Lucas got up out of his seat in the front row, came back to his father, and hugged him. It was a movie moment.

Lucas may not have *learned all the stuff*, but he had succeeded. You don't need to know all the right stuff to have an impact on your world. But you've got to have desire. Lucas has a fire for God in his eyes that I want. Lucas Brown. Remember that name.

He's already an incredible man of God.

Nick's Story

LUIS PALAU

When Nick called, he was a man on the run, desperate, lonely, with a gun and two bullets. He would need only one....

For fifteen years Nick moved with the Mexican Mafia, dealing drugs in East Los Angeles. He earned ten thousand dollars a week. Sometimes fifteen thousand. But his wife and three children left him. One brother was in prison. Two friends and a cousin were dead.

"You'd better get out of here 'cause you're not doin' nothin' with your life," his father counseled. "You'll just end up like your cousin."

Nick took his father's advice and boarded a bus to Tulsa. Six months later, with no friends, no steady job, and mounting pressure from Mafia buddies to return to Los Angeles, Nick was ready to end his life.

The gun lay on a table in his apartment. Nervously surfing through channels on TV, he stopped to listen to *Night Talk,* our call-in counseling program broadcast each evening that week during the Greater Tulsa Crusade. Thinking I was a psychologist, Nick called the number on the screen. By the time he was put through to me on the air, Nick had watched as I prayed with two others who had called.

"I just want to know, maybe you think God might be able to help me?" he asked. And he told me his story. My heart melted with compassion. I advised him to change his phone number to stop the calls from old buddies, and I promised to put him in touch with Christian men his age who could encourage him.

Most of all, he needed the Lord. "Tonight, Nick, are you ready to open your heart to Christ?" I asked

"Do you think He could help me?"

"Absolutely. The Lord wants to come into your life. Christ died on the cross for you, Nick. He took away all the guilt and shame of the things you've done and paid the punishment that you and I deserve. If the law caught up with you dealing drugs, they would come down hard. The law hasn't caught you, but the Lord has. Instead of nailing you, the Lord says, 'Nick, I love you.'

"Christ is calling you, knocking at the door of your heart. If you say, 'Yes, Lord Jesus, I don't understand it all, but I want You to come into my life,' you're going to see a change that you won't believe. In a year you'll be a different man, filled with joy and contentment. You'll have different goals in life, different dreams. You'll have power to overcome temptation. Christ will really change your life, but you must open your heart to Him, and I'd like to help you do that.

In the next moments, Nick received Christ as his Savior. He threw his gun into the river the next day and that evening came with one of my team members to the crusade rally, saying he felt like a new man.

"Nick, you are a new man," I assured him as the Convention Center crowd welcomed him with rousing applause.

Several months later, Nick moved again—to a place far from Los Angeles. He found steady work in landscaping and accountable fellowship at a good church.

"I haven't carried a gun in a year," he told our team members when he visited our association's Center for World Evangelism. "I'm working, which I have never really done before. I read the Bible and pray—just sit down and talk to God. If people think I'm crazy, I don't care...I don't care if they laugh at me. I used to get angry. If somebody even looked at me bad, I'd have beat him up. There are times when I felt like giving up, and then I think, *No, I've gone too far. Don't give up now.* I know God is with me."

Later, I received this letter from Nick:

You know, Dr. Palau, the other day I was sitting down at the dinner table, and my son looked at me and out of the blue asked me a question I never thought would come out of my child's mouth. He said to me, "Dad, I know you're not going out with your old friends anymore or doing drugs and stuff like that. But are you happy with yourself because sometimes I see you sad. Are you mad because we're here?"

At that moment, I thought back to what my life was and what my kids and wife had gone through with me. Remembered that since the time I was my son's age, twelve years old, I had been involved in the gang life. They were everything to me. As I sat there looking at him I thought back to Tulsa, Oklahoma. And I told him I wasn't sad, but happy to be with them and would never want it any other way.

What I'm trying to say is thank you for not only showing me the way to Jesus Christ, but also showing me there are people out there that do care about guys like me. I feel like God has given me another chance in life to be the father and the husband that my family deserves. I guess He was always there for me, but I really didn't seek Him out....

I know and pray that more people like myself will make it out. If you could do me one big favor; please tell the young teenagers that you meet up with that it's not worth it to get into gangs. We have to get to them now because it's hard to reach them when they are older. Let them know there is always a way out. Just tell them about me.

I believe Nick is going to make it. Not because of me, or anything I said. He's going to make it because he now has the Spirit of God Himself at work in his life. And teens, Lord willing, you have a whole lot of life ahead of you, too.

Take on an entirely new way of life—
a God-fashioned life, a life renewed from the inside
and working itself into your conduct as God reproduces his character in you.

EPHESIANS 4:24
THE MESSAGE

The Transformation of Big "T"

TONY T. NELSON
AS TOLD TO TERRY ARRIES

s a boy, I learned to look out for myself; I learned not to feel, not to care. I learned to survive—and to hate. My father was a military man and a very hard person, physically and emotionally. He said that if ever I hit him, he would kill me. I believed him, so I never tried.

But that didn't stop him from making my life agony. When I was fifteen, my mother finally left him. She had to work three jobs to support us kids. I told myself that I'd never again back down from a fight. But I had a deep emptiness inside me. I could not assuage my anger over life. Contentment and peace eluded me.

It was easy for me to get money on the streets. I could get what I wanted and take what I wanted; nobody could stop me. I stayed in drugs and out of school. The hollowness in my soul gnawed at me. I knew that I needed to straighten out my life, so I went into the U.S. Army. I learned that military life did not help ease the hellish emptiness inside me. Being able to get high and get other people high gave me status. I could have any girl I wanted. I was Big Tony, Big "T." I was 6'2" and 300 pounds, and people learned to stay out of my way.

When I got out of the Army, I trained a group of people in the drills and the tactics that I had learned in the Army. I brought together this group of people to take over drug and prostitution territories in Denver, Colorado, and taught them to be ruthless. I made sure that they understood that I was the most important individual in any room, and if I were ever wounded, I would kill whoever was supposed to have protected me.

Soon I was on the run from the police—I'd broken into a sporting goods store to steal guns, but the store had been robbed before, and now all the guns were securely locked. I saw a video camera on a tripod and thought that it was a demonstration model. Not wanting to leave empty-handed, I took the camera.

But the camera was attached to a VCR that had videotaped everything I had done in the store— one of my guys called me and said, "'T,' you've got to leave; your picture is all over television."

I packed a few things and was on the run. I felt stupid to be so easily identified on the tape. How long could I avoid the police? Nothing lay ahead of me but being caged up for years. My conscience battered me. I felt ashamed at the way that I had lived my life, of the things that I had done. With weariness of soul, I stopped to see Momma May, a family friend I had known when I was a child in Colorado Springs.

"Momma's been praying for you for years," she said tenderly. "I want you to promise Momma to read this book." Momma May handed me a small Bible.

So there I was on a bus—all 300 pounds of me—reading this Bible. I was hunkered down in my bus seat and used a small flashlight to read the Bible. I was in a maelstrom of conviction about how I was living my life. I asked myself questions and found the answers in the Book. I tried to focus on the words, sniffling all the while.

In Seattle, Washington, I held temporary jobs and kept reading my Bible every day. I couldn't put it down, and I couldn't stop crying. All the tears that had been pent up over the years came out. I was being cleansed by the Living Water of the Word.

One day, in a dingy little apartment in Seattle, I turned to the back of my Bible where I found a prayer of salvation. I prayed that prayer and asked Jesus Christ to be my Savior and Lord. He heard my heart's cry, and the hunger and the emptiness that I'd carried all my life was heard—I became a new creature in Christ. My battered soul was loved back to life and hope.

I knew what I had to do. I moved back to Denver and gave the police a signed written confession and a videotaped confession of my crime. God performed a miracle and kept me out of prison; the judge gave me probation.

Yet, my old habits still had a hold on me. I was surrounded by my former companions, and I relapsed into crime and subsequently served seven years in prison. There I sought God with my whole heart. I spent time reading my Bible and in prayer with God. I never wanted to fall away from Him again. One day it seemed as if He said to me, "If you will obey Me, I will provide a way for you." God granted me His favor, and while I was still in prison, I started to minister to others. This has remained the focus of my life in the years following my release. God gave me 1 Corinthians 2:9 as my life verse: "As it is written, Eye hath not seen, nor ear heard, neither have entered into the heart of man, the things which God hath prepared for them that love him" (King James Version). How faithfully God has fulfilled these words in my life!

Upon my release from prison, I was taken to a halfway house in Durango, Colorado. There I met Janet Embree, who worked with her pastor and her church in bringing the hope of Jesus Christ to men struggling to regain their lives in society.

Janet and I married, and three years later

we started an evangelistic ministry. People from many different congregations help us in our ministry to reach kids and adults in trouble. We also work in community programs and in nursing homes, telling people about Jesus.

I talk with kids and try to teach them the spiritual skills to live in the world and to be leaders for the future. Then I encourage them to go back to their churches and say, "We would like to help in the nursery today or help teach Sunday school. Maybe we can help with cleaning."

When I meet people, I want them to see that there is something different about me. When they ask me about it, I let them know it is not something—but Someone!

Those who become Christians become new persons.
They are not the same anymore, for the old life is gone.
A new life has begun!

2 CORINTHIANS 5:17
NEW LIVING TRANSLATION

Phil Joel of the Newsboys

KIM CLAASSEN
FROM *LUIS PALAU EVANGELISTIC ASSOCIATION*

P hil Joel is well known in the music world. He plays bass for the Newsboys, a contemporary Christian music group originally from Down Under that has sold millions of albums here in America. The whole course of his life changed one day while he was growing up in New Zealand:

> I remember when I was 14 and a Luis Palau crusade was coming up, and I knew I was going to it with a youth group I was hanging out with. I didn't really know much about it. All I knew was what would happen at the end. It was going to be an invitation of, "Do you want to follow Christ or not?" So I went with that idea in mind.
>
> I had been involved with church here and there, and my family were churchgoing people. Up until I was 14, I didn't really know what I was doing; didn't really know if I would follow Christ, or if the world was more fun than being a Christian. Or even if this whole Christianity stuff actually made any sense.
>
> But I knew if the stuff at the crusade made sense, and if this guy, Luis Palau, made sense about the Gospel, and made sense in what he presented, then I was going to go for it.

*A friend and I went forward that night. And I remember know-
ing, really knowing, that this was it. That night was a landmark in
my life. And I had to follow this Jesus, this whole Christianity bit, to
the end.*

Today, Phil and his band tour the world and occasionally team up with
evangelist Luis Palau to present "Great Music and Good News" to huge audi-
ences across America and around the globe. Phil's doing exactly what he
decided as a teen—following Jesus to the end. And he's pointing hundreds
of thousands of other young people in the same direction.

faith

Open Windows

Faith goes up the stairs that love had made
and looks out the window which hope has opened.

CHARLES SPURGEON

Table for Two

WAYNE RICE
FROM *STILL MORE HOT ILLUSTRATIONS*
FOR YOUTH TALKS

h e sits by himself at a table for two.

The uniformed waiter returns to his side and asks, "Would you like to go ahead and order, sir?" The man has, after all, been waiting since seven o'clock—almost half an hour. "No, thank you," the man smiles. "I'll wait for her a while longer. How about some more coffee?"

"Certainly, sir."

The man sits, his clear blue eyes gazing straight through the flowered centerpiece. He fingers his napkin, allowing the sounds of light chatter, tinkling silverware, and mellow music to fill his mind. He is dressed in sport coat and tie. His dark brown hair is neatly combed, but one stray lock insists on dropping to his forehead. The scent of his cologne adds to his clean-cut image. He is dressed up enough to make a companion feel important, respected, loved. Yet he is not so formal as to make one uncomfortable. It seems that he has taken every precaution to make others feel at ease with him. Still, he sits alone.

The waiter returns to fill the man's coffee cup. "Is there anything else I can get for you, sir?"

"No, thank you."

The waiter remains standing at the table. Something tugs at his curiosity.

"I don't mean to pry, but…" His voice trails off. This line of conversation could jeopardize his tip.

"Go ahead," the man encourages. His voice is strong, yet sensitive, inviting conversation.

"Why do you bother waiting for her?" the waiter finally blurts out. This man has been at the restaurant other evenings, always patiently alone. Says the man quietly, "Because she needs me."

"Are you sure?"

"Yes."

"Well, sir, no offense, but assuming that she needs you, she sure isn't acting much like it. She's stood you up three times just this week."

The man winces, and looks down at the table. "Yes, I know."

"Then why do you still come here and wait?"

"Cassie said that she would be here."

"She's said that before," the waiter protests. "I wouldn't put up with it. Why do you?"

Now the man looks up, smiles at the waiter, and says simply, "Because I love her."

The waiter walks away, wondering how one could love a girl who stands him up three times a week. The man must be crazy, he decides. Across the room, he turns to look at the man again. The man slowly pours cream into his coffee. He twirls his spoon between his fingers a few times before stirring sweetener into his cup. After staring for a moment into the liquid, the man brings the cup to his mouth and sips, silently watching those around him. He doesn't look crazy, the waiter admits. Maybe the girl has qualities that I don't know about. Or maybe the man's love is stronger than most. The waiter shakes himself out of his musings to take an order from a party of five.

The man watches the waiter, wonders if he's ever been stood up. The man has, many times. But he still can't get used to it. Each time, it hurts. He's looked forward to this evening all day. He has many things, exciting things, to tell Cassie. But, more importantly, he wants to hear Cassie's voice. He wants her to tell him all about her day, her triumphs, her defeats…anything, really. He has tried so many times to show Cassie how much he loves her. He'd just like to know that she cares for him, too. He sips sporadically at the coffee, and loses himself in thought, knowing that Cassie is late, but still hoping that she will arrive.

The clock says nine-thirty when the waiter returns to the man's table. "Is there anything I can get for you?"

The still empty chair stabs at the man. "No, I think that will be all for tonight. May I have the check please?"

"Yes, sir."

When the waiter leaves, the man picks up the check. He pulls out his wallet and sighs. He has enough money to have given Cassie a feast. But he takes out only enough to pay for his five cups of coffee and the tip. *Why do you do this, Cassie,* his mind cries as he gets up from the table.

"Good-bye," the waiter says, as the man walks towards the door.

"Good night. Thank you for your service."

"You're welcome, sir," says the waiter softly, for he sees the hurt in the man's eyes that his smile doesn't hide.

The man passes a laughing young couple on his way out, and his eyes glisten as he thinks of the good time he and Cassie could have had. He stops at the front and makes reservations for tomorrow. Maybe Cassie will be able to make it, he thinks.

"Seven o'clock tomorrow for party of two?" the hostess confirms.

"That's right," the man replies.

"Do you think she'll come?" asks the hostess. She doesn't mean to be rude, but she has watched the man many times alone at his table for two.

"Someday, yes. And I will be

waiting for her." The man buttons his overcoat and walks out of the restaurant, alone. His shoulders are hunched, but through the windows the hostess can only guess whether they are hunched against the wind or against the man's hurt.

As the man turns toward home, Cassie turns into bed. She is tired after an evening out with friends. As she reaches toward her nightstand to set the alarm, she sees the note that she scribbled to herself. *7:00*, it says. *Spend some time in prayer.* Darn, she thinks. She forgot again. She feels a twinge of guilt, but quickly pushes it aside. She needed that time with her friends. And now she needs her sleep. She can pray tomorrow night. Jesus will forgive her.

And she's sure He doesn't mind.

Look! I stand at the door and knock.
If you hear me calling and open the door,
I will come in, and we will share a meal as friends.

REVELATION 3:20
NEW LIVING TRANSLATION

Miracles

YITTA HALBERSTAM AND JUDITH LEVENTHAL
FROM *SMALL MIRACLES II*

L ife's a little thing! Robert Browning once wrote. But a little thing can mean a life. Even two lives. How well I remember. Two years ago in downtown Denver my friend, Scott Reasoner, and I saw a tiny and insignificant event change the world, but no one else even seemed to notice.

It was one of those beautiful Denver days. Crystal clear and no humidity, not a cloud in the sky. We decided to walk the ten blocks to an outdoor restaurant rather than take the shuttle bus that runs up and down the Sixteenth Street Mall. The restaurant, in the shape of a baseball diamond, was called The Blake Street Baseball Club. Tables were set appropriately on the grass infield. Many colorful pennants and flags hung limply overhead.

As we sat outside, the sun continued to beat down on us, and it became increasingly hot. There wasn't a hint of a breeze, and the heat radiated up from the tabletop. Nothing moved, except the waiters, of course. And they didn't move very fast.

After lunch Scott and I started to walk back up the mall. We both noticed a young mother and her daughter walking out of a card shop toward the street. She was holding her daughter by the hand while reading a greeting card. It was immediately apparent to us that she was so engrossed in the card that she did not notice a shuttle bus moving toward her at a good clip.

She and her daughter were one step away from disaster when Scott started to yell. He hadn't even got a word out when a breeze blew the card out of her hand and over her shoulder. She spun around and grabbed the card nearly knocking her daughter over. By the time she picked up the card from the ground and turned back to cross the street, the shuttle bus had whizzed by her. She never knew what almost happened.

To this day, two things continue to perplex me about this event. Where did that one spurt of wind come from to blow the card out of that young mother's hand? There had not been a whisper of wind at lunch, or during our long walk back up to the mall. Secondly, if Scott had been able to get his words out, the young mother might have looked up at us as they continued to walk into the bus. It was the wind that made her turn back to the card—in the direction that saved her life and that of her daughter. The passing bus did not create the wind. On the contrary, the wind came from the opposite direction.

I have no doubt it was a breath from God protecting them both. But the awesomeness of this miracle is that she never knew. As we continued back to work, I wondered at how God often acts in our lives without our being aware. The difference between life and death can very well be a little thing.

Miracles often blow unseen through our lives!

The Story of Her Life

KIM CLAASSEN

FROM *LUIS PALAU EVANGELISTIC ASSOCIATION*

bye, Mom!" Paul yelled as he ran out the door to meet his girlfriend, Tiffany Phillips, and some other friends. It was one of those spontaneous Sunday afternoons when the world belongs to those who grasp it—and today, that meant a group of five teenagers.

Just an hour earlier, Tiffany had joined Seaside Christian Church, wanting the world to know of her love for Jesus Christ. Her life had been good, with parents who loved her and cared for her. She excelled in track and volleyball, loved her friends and knew they loved her. But nothing could equal that moment when she trusted Christ as her Savior, knowing He gently held her life and heart in His hand.

Now she was off to celebrate that life with a group of friends as they headed for the Tillamook cheese factory to have ice cream and shop in the gift store. When they stopped to pick up two more friends, Tiffany undid her seat belt and slid into the middle of the back seat, next to Paul. Then they headed off down Highway 101, loudly singing songs from the movie Grease, not minding the sporadic Oregon rain.

Rounding a slight curve moments later, the songs died as Tiffany's friend Jeremy lost control of the Subaru. They slid across the centerline, into the path of an on-coming pickup. Jeremy automatically clutched the steering wheel and braced himself as the 1979 pickup hit them on their rear corner. The Subaru turned enough to clip the truck once again. Then, as they spun 360 degrees into the oncoming traffic, a 1993 Aerostar van slammed into the Subaru's left side, crushing the three teenagers in the back seat.

Paul knew nothing else until medics strapped him onto a gurney. He didn't yet realize that in that moment of eternity, four lives changed and one life that truly had just begun was ended.

The next morning, students at Seaside High School returned to classes for the first day after Christmas break. They yelled to each other across hallways, asking about Christmas presents and winter holiday fun. Some noticed the quiet huddles of students in a classroom or hall. Some heard rumors, but couldn't quite believe the news.

Half an hour later, incredulous silence filled the school's halls. The principal had announced Tiffany's death and the injuries of the other four friends in the car with her. Everyone knew Tiffany. Some were in band with her, where she had played the trombone for four years. Others ran in track or played volleyball with her. Friends had walked with her to her parents' candy store downtown, even managing to get free samples on days they needed extra encouragement. Some had worked with her on Pacific Project, a senior year community project, putting together food baskets for needy people. All of them had seen her smile, heard her encouraging words. "She was the first person I met who wasn't afraid to love anybody," student Josh Lively would later say.

Being the good kid she was, Tiffany's life had not changed drastically when she trusted Jesus Christ as her Savior at the Winter Youth celebration. She simply decided at that point that everything she did would be for God's glory and purpose.

Tiffany was a girl who asked questions and thought through her decisions. A few months earlier, she had attended the Luis Palau Coastal Crusade with her boyfriend Paul. "She sat in the front row at Youth Night and fully participated," Paul's mom said. "But she didn't go forward then."

Mike Hague and Terry O'Casey, youth and senior pastors at Seaside Christian Church, helped answer some of Tiffany's questions one evening. Still, she wasn't ready to publicly commit her life to Jesus Christ.

But at Winter Youth she was ready to give her life to God. On a Sunday morning January fourth, she was ready to tell the rest of the world. Her mother sat in the church congregation, happy to see her daughter making her statement of faith. She couldn't have known how much it would mean to her in the days and weeks that followed.

Tiffany's public statement of trust in Jesus Christ quickly traveled beyond the church walls. The services of Seaside Christian Church were videotaped and broadcast on the local cable network. The high school showed the video every day the following week. All week long students filled the library to hear her testimony.

God continued to use Tiffany's life to touch others' lives. At Seaside Christian Church the next Sunday morning, her best friend Juliet and twelve more youth and adults walked the same aisle Tiffany had walked a week earlier. They, too, surrendered their lives to the gentle, loving hands of Jesus Christ.

Boxes

Author unknown

I have in my hands two boxes
Which God gave me to hold.
He said, "Put all your sorrows in the black,
And all your joys in the gold."

I heeded His words, and in the two boxes
Both my joys and sorrows I store.
But though the gold became heavier each day
The black was as light as before.

With curiosity, I opened the black
I wanted to find out why.
And I saw, in the base of the box, a hole
Which my sorrows had fallen out by.

I showed the hole to God, and mused aloud,
"I wonder where my sorrows could be."
He smiled a gentle smile at me,
"My child, they're all here with me."

I asked, "God, why give me the boxes,
Why the gold, and the black with the hole?"
"My child, the gold is for you to count your blessings,
The black is for you to let go."

Precious Sacrifice

BILLY GRAHAM
FROM *UNTO THE HILLS*

loving mother once saved her little girl from a burning house, but suffered severe burns on her hands and arms. When the girl grew up, not knowing how her mother's arms became so seared, she was ashamed of the scarred, gnarled hands and always insisted that her mother wear long gloves to cover up that ugliness.

But one day the daughter asked her mother how her hands became so scarred. For the first time the mother told her the story of how she had saved her life with those hands. The daughter wept tears of gratitude and said, "Oh Mother, those are beautiful hands, the most beautiful in the world. Don't ever hide them again."

The blood of Christ may seem to be a grim and repulsive subject to those who do not realize its true significance, but to those who have accepted His redemption and have been set free from the slavery of sin, the blood of Christ is precious.

He is so rich in kindness that he purchased our freedom
through the blood of his Son, and our sins are forgiven.

EPHESIANS 1:7
NEW LIVING TRANSLATION

A Vital Decision

HELEN HAIDLE

"Rabouka!" called Mother urgently. "It's important that you help get dinner ready. We must not be late for prayer meeting tonight."

A tall, slender girl stepped in the door of the New Guinea hut. "But I'm studying for finals at school. The tests are given tomorrow. I must do well on them if I want to attend classes in Papua premedical school next year. Can't I stay home tonight? I'll go to the prayer meeting tomorrow night."

Mother looked up from stirring the soup. Her eyes grew sad. "It's up to you, dear. I wish you could have been here when Pastor came by this afternoon. He told us that it was God, not him, who had called this prayer meeting tonight at church. Pastor has never said anything like this before. I feel that there is an urgent reason why we must be there—all of us."

Rabouka brushed her long hair back from her face. She struggled with her decision. She loved her studies...but she also loved her pastor. She knew that it must be important if he called them to prayer on a Tuesday night when the regular prayer service was always held Wednesday night.

She sat down at the table and opened her notebook. *I know God wants me to become a doctor someday and help my people. These tests are important for my acceptance into medical school.* She looked out the window and listened to the birds. *Yes, little songbirds. I'll try not to worry about the future. God will help me with my studies...and my grades.*

The decision weighed heavy on the teenager's heart as she finished her science review. *Dear God*, she prayed, *Help me trust Your promise that, when I seek first Your Kingdom, everything I need shall be given to me. I will go to prayer meeting tonight. And I will trust You to help me with my math when I return.*

"Okay, Mother. I'll come, too. If God spoke to Pastor, we should do as he says. Perhaps I can study some more when we return from prayer meeting. I'm just not sure if I can go to church two nights in a row."

"Then go tonight instead of tomorrow night," urged Mother. "Somehow I feel that this is more important."

After supper, Rabouka and her parents climbed the hill to their church built on stilts. For over two hours they lifted their voices and their hands in worship and prayer to the Lord.

"I am glad we came," Rabouka whispered to her mother. "I feel Jesus' presence stronger than I ever have in my life."

Soon Rabouka felt something else, something wet and cold around her bare feet. She looked down to see water quickly rising to her ankles. "Mother!" she whispered. "What is happening? Why is the floor wet?"

Others noticed the cold water also. Everyone stopped singing.

"Stay calm," said Pastor. He slowly shoved open the door of the church. In the light of his lantern they saw swirling floodwater completely surrounding their church building.

While they had worshiped and prayed that evening, an enormous tidal wave smashed against the northern coast of New Guinea. The force of the water washed all the houses and the people of Rabouka's village out to sea. Only the people in Rabouka's little church that stood on the hill were alive and safe.

And you will hear a voice say,
"This is the way; turn around and walk here."

Isaiah 30:21, New Living Translation

Seeing God

AUTHOR UNKNOWN

a young man was desperately seeking God. He sought out a wise old man who lived in a nearby beach house and posed the question: "Old man, how can I see God?" The old man who obviously knew God at a depth few of us experience, pondered the question for a very long time. At last he responded quietly: "Young man, I am not sure that I can help you— for you see, I have a very different problem. I cannot NOT see him."

Dear Friend

AUTHOR UNKNOWN

ear Friend,
How are you?

I just had to send you a note to tell you how much I care about you

I saw you yesterday as you were talking with your friends.... I waited all day, hoping you would want to talk with me too.

I gave you a delightful sunset to close your day, and to rest you.... I waited, but you never talked to me. It hurt me, but I still love you because you are my friend.

I saw you sleeping last night and longed to touch your brow, so I spilled moonlight upon your face. Again I waited, wanting to rush down so we could talk. I have so many gifts for you! I love you!

You awoke and rushed off to your daily activities. My tears were in the rain.

If you would only listen to me! I love you! I try to tell you in the deep blue sky and in the stillness of the night. I whisper my love to you in the quietness of the silent snow, shout it in the mountain streams. I give the birds songs to sing to you. I clothe you in fresh, clean air filled with the scents of nature.

My love for you is deeper than the ocean and bigger than the deepest need in your heart!

Ask me! Talk with me! Please don't forget me! I have so much to share with you!

I won't bother you any further. It is your decision. I have chosen you and I will wait.

I love you.

Your friend,

Jesus

Mandy's Story

LUIS PALAU

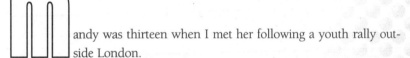andy was thirteen when I met her following a youth rally outside London.

She told me her father, a famous jazz musician, and her mother, a well-known British television personality, were divorced. They never attended church, never talked about God, and didn't even own a Bible.

Mandy said she had never heard about Jesus Christ. But when she learned that Jesus died for her sins on a Roman cross, rose again, and was coming back to take all those who believed in Him to heaven, she prayed with me and invited Jesus into her heart.

As we neared the end of our discussion, I showed her what Jesus says to all believers in John 10:28: "I give them eternal life, and they shall never perish; no one can snatch them out of my hand."

She said, "That's what I have now."

As the months passed, Mandy began to tell others what Jesus Christ had done for her. She told her family and her school friends that she knew for certain she was going to heaven when she died.

Three years later the phone call came. Mandy had gone on a date three days before her sixteenth birthday. It had begun to drizzle and the car swerved out of control and crashed. Mandy's date was thrown clear of the convertible and was uninjured. But Mandy died instantly.

Mandy's parents asked me to give the sermon at her funeral service because they said, "Mandy talked so much about Jesus, going to heaven, and her friend, Luis Palau."

On the day of the funeral, the church was filled with famous personalities, all of who had a view of the casket that contained Mandy's body, "Ladies and gentlemen," I said to these famous people, "what you see in the casket is not Mandy. It is Mandy's body, but the real Mandy is not here. Mandy is in heaven with Jesus Christ because the Bible says, 'away from the body and at home with the Lord'" (2 Corinthians 5:8).

Then I said to them, "We're going to bury Mandy's body this afternoon. But the Bible says that the body is just the house of the soul and spirit; the essence or who we really are. Because Mandy had eternal life through Jesus Christ, she went straight to heaven when she died. Although her body will stay here, her soul and spirit went immediately to be with the Lord."

Compared to eternal life, all other decisions aren't that important when you think about it. C. S. Lewis wrote: "No one is ready to live life on earth until he is ready for life in heaven." We don't normally think about it that way, but it's true.

Mandy was prepared for her trip into eternity. Are you?

God gave us eternal life; the life is in his Son.
So, whoever has the Son, has life;
whoever rejects the Son, rejects life.

1 JOHN 5:11–13
THE MESSAGE

Safely Home

JOAN WESTER ANDERSON

t was just past midnight on December 24, 1983. The Midwest was shivering through a record-breaking cold spell, complete with gale-force winds and frozen water pipes. And although our suburban Chicago household was filled with the snug sounds of a family at rest, I couldn't be a part of them, not until our twenty-one-year-old son pulled into the driveway. At the moment, Tim and his two roommates were driving home for Christmas, their first trip back since they had moved East, last May.

"Don't worry, Mom," Tim had reassured me over the phone last night. "We're going to leave before dawn tomorrow and drive straight through. We'll be fine!"

Kids. They do insane things. Under normal circumstances, I figured, a Connecticut-to-Illinois trek ought to take about eighteen hours. But the weather had turned so dangerously cold that radio reports warned against venturing outdoors, even for a few moments. And we had heard nothing from the travelers. Distressed, I pictured them on a desolate road. What if they ran into car problems or lost their way? And if they *had* been delayed, why hadn't Tim phoned? Restlessly I paced and prayed in the familiar shorthand all mothers know: *God, send someone to help them.*

By now, as I later learned, the trio had stopped briefly in Fort Wayne, Indiana, to deposit Don at his family home. Common sense suggested that Tim and Jim stay the rest of the night and resume their trek in the morning. But when does common sense prevail with invincible young adults? There were only four driving hours left to reach home. And although it was the coldest night in Midwest history and the highways were snowy and deserted, the two had started out again.

They had been traveling for only a few miles on a rural access road to the Indiana tollway, when they noticed that the car's engine seemed sluggish, lurching erratically and dying to ten or fifteen miles per hour. Tim glanced uneasily at Jim. "Do not—" the radio announcer intoned, "repeat—do *not* venture outside tonight, friends. There's a record wind-chill of eighty below zero, which means that exposed skin will freeze in less than a minute." The car surged suddenly, then coughed and slowed again.

"Tim," Jim spoke into the darkness, "we're not going to stall here, are we?"

"We can't," Tim answered grimly as he pumped the accelerator. "We'd die for sure."

But instead of picking up speed, the engine sputtered, chugging and slowing again. About a mile later, at the top of a small incline, the car crawled to a frozen stop.

Horrified, Tim and Jim looked at each other in the darkened interior. They could see across the fields in every direction, but, incredibly, theirs was the only vehicle in view. For the first time, they faced the fact that they were in enormous danger. There was no traffic, no refuge ahead, not even a farmhouse light blinking in the distance. It was as if they had landed on an alien, snow-covered planet.

And the appalling, unbelievable cold! Never in Tim's life had he experienced anything so intense. They couldn't run for help; he knew that for sure. He and Jim were young and strong, but even if shelter were only a short distance away they couldn't survive. The temperature would kill them in a matter of minutes.

"Someone will come along soon," Jim muttered, looking in every direction. "They're bound to."

"I don't think so," Tim said. "You heard the radio. Everyone in the world is inside tonight—except us."

"Then what are we going to do?"

"I don't know." Tim tried starting the engine again, but the ignition key clicked hopelessly in the silence. Bone-chilling cold penetrated the car's interior, and his feet were already growing numb. *Well, God,* he prayed, echoing my own distant plea, *You're the only one who can help us now.*

It seemed impossible to stay awake much longer.... Then, as if they had already slipped into a dream, they saw headlights flashing at the car's rear. But that was impossible. For they had seen no twin pinpricks of light in the distance, no hopeful approach. Where had the vehicle come from? Had they already died?

But no. For, miraculously, someone was knocking on the driver's side window, "Need to be pulled?" In disbelief they heard the muffled shout. But it was true. Their rescuer was driving a tow truck.

"Yes! Oh, yes, thanks!" Quickly, the two conferred as the driver, saying nothing more, drove around to the front of the car and attached chains. If there were no garages open at this hour, they would ask him to take them back to Don's house, where they could spend the rest of the night.

Swathed almost completely in a furry parka, hood and a scarf up to his eyes, the driver nodded at their request but said nothing more. He was calm, they noted as he climbed into his truck, seemingly unconcerned about the life-threatening circumstances in which he had found them. *Strange that he's not curious about us,* Tim mused, *and isn't even explaining where he came from or how he managed to approach without our seeing him....* And had there been lettering on the side of the truck? Tim hadn't noticed any. *He's going to give us a big bill, on a night like this. I'll have to borrow some money from Don or his dad....* But Tim was exhausted from the ordeal, and gradually, as he leaned against the seat, his thoughts slipped away.

They passed two locked service stations, stopped to alert Don from a pay phone, and were soon being towed back through the familiar Fort Wayne neighborhood. Hushed, Christmas lights long since extinguished and families asleep, Don's still seemed the most welcoming street they had ever been on. The driver maneuvered carefully around the cul-de-sac and pulled up in front of Don's house. Numb with cold, Tim and Jim raced to the side door where Don was waiting, then tumbled into the blessedly warm kitchen, safe at last.

"The tow truck driver, Don—have to pay him. I need to borrow—"

"Wait a minute." Don frowned, looking past his friends through the window. "I don't see any tow truck out there."

Tim and Jim turned around. There, parked alone at the curb was Tim's car. There had been no sound in the crystal-clear night of its release from the chains, no door slam, no chug of an engine pulling away. There had been no bill for Tim to pay, no receipt to sign, no farewell or "thank you" or "Merry Christmas."

Stunned, Tim raced back down the driveway to the curb, but there were no taillights disappearing in the distance, no engine noise echoing through the silent streets, nothing at all to mark the tow truck's presence.

Then Tim saw the tire tracks traced in the windblown snowdrifts. But there was only one set of marks ringing the cul-de-sac curve. And they belonged to Tim's car....

For he orders his angels to protect you wherever you go.

PSALM 91:11
NEW LIVING TRANSLATION

The Cost

PHILIP YANCEY
FROM *WHAT'S SO AMAZING ABOUT GRACE?*

In the movie *The Last Emperor*, the young child anointed as the last emperor of China lives in a magical life of luxury with a thousand eunuch servants at his command. "What happens when you do wrong?" his brother asks. "When I do wrong, someone else is punished," the boy emperor replies. To demonstrate, he breaks a jar, and one of the servants is beaten.

In Christian theology, Jesus reversed that ancient pattern: when the servants erred, the King was punished, Grace is free only because the giver himself has borne the cost.

The Song

NATHAN S. ABRAMS
AN EIGHTH-GRADE HOMESCHOOL STUDENT
FROM *DECISION* MAGAZINE

The sound of the whip on His fair back,
A cry!
  The song of pain.

  Pushing the thorns onto His head,
  A gasp!
  The song of suffering.

  Spitting, jeering, mocking, cursing,
  A slap!
  The song of despair.

  Hammer striking, nails cold and cruel,
  A ring!
  The song of sorrow.

  Thunder, lightning, rolling away the stone,
  A flash!
  The song of victory.

 Pain, despair, death, victory,
A promise!
The song of eternal life.

Cosmic Christmas

MAX LUCADO
FROM *COSMIC CHRISTMAS*

gabriel."

Just the sound of my King's voice stirred my heart. I left my post at the entryway and stepped into the throne room. To my left was the desk on which sat the Book of Life. Ahead of me was the throne of Almighty God. I entered the circle of unceasing Light, folded my wings before me to cover my face, and knelt before Him. "Yes, my Lord?"

"You have served the kingdom well. You are a noble messenger. Never have you flinched in duty. Never have you flagged in zeal."

I bowed my head, basking in the words. "Whatever You ask, I'll do a thousand times over, my King," I promised.

"Of that I have no doubt, dear messenger." His voice assumed a solemnity I'd never heard Him use. "But your greatest work lies ahead of you. Your next assignment is to carry a gift to Earth. Behold."

I lifted my eyes to see a necklace, a clear vial on a golden chain dangling from His extended hand.

My Father spoke earnestly, "Though empty, this vial will soon contain My greatest gift. Place it around your neck."

I was about to take it when a raspy voice interrupted me. "And what treasure will You send to Earth this time?"

My back stiffened at the irreverent tone, and my stomach turned at the sudden stench. Such foul odor could only come from one being. I drew my sword and turned to do battle with Lucifer. The Father's hand on my shoulder stopped me.

"Worry not, Gabriel. He will do no harm."

I stepped back and stared at God's enemy. He was completely covered. A black cassock hung over his skeletal frame, hiding his body and arms and hooding his face. The feet, protruding beneath the robe, were thrice-toed and clawed. The skin on his hands was that of a snake. Talons extended from his fingers. He pulled his cape further over his face as a shield against the Light, but the brightness still pained him. Seeking relief, he turned toward me. I caught a glimpse of a skullish face within the cowl.

"What are you staring at, Gabriel?" he sneered. "Are you that glad to see me?"

I had no words for this fallen angel. Both what I saw and what I remembered left me speechless. I remembered him before the Rebellion: Poised proudly at the vanguard of our force, wings wide, holding forth a radiant sword, he had inspired us to do the same. Who could refuse him? The sight of his velvet hair and coal-black eyes had far outstripped the beauty of any celestial being.

Any being, of course, except our Creator. No one compared Lucifer to God—except Lucifer. How he came to think he was worthy of the same worship as God, only God knows. All I knew was that I had not seen Satan since the Rebellion. And what I now saw repulsed me.

I searched for just a hint of his former splendor but saw none.

"Your news must be urgent," spat Satan to God, still unable to bear the Light.

My Father's response was a pronouncement. "The time has come for the second gift."

The frame beneath the cape bounced stiffly as Lucifer chuckled. "The second gift, eh? I hope it works better than the first."

"You're disappointed with the first?" asked the Father.

"Oh, quite the contrary; I've delighted in it." Lifting a bony finger, he spelled a word in the air: C-H-O-I-C-E.

"You gave Adam his choice," Satan scoffed. "And what a choice he made! He chose me. Ever since the fruit was plucked from the tree in the Garden, I've held Your children captive. They fell. Fast. Hard. They are mine. You have failed. Heh-heh-heh."

"You speak so confidently," replied the Father, astounding me with His patience.

Lucifer stepped forward, his cloak dragging behind him. "Of course! I thwart everything You do! You soften hearts, I harden them. You teach truth, I shadow it. You offer joy, I steal it."

He pivoted and paraded around the room, boasting of his deeds. "The betrayal of Joseph by his brothers—I did that. Moses banished to the desert after killing the Egyptian—I did that. David watching Bathsheba bathe—that was me. You must admit, my work has been crafty."

Crafty? Perhaps. But effective? No. I know what you will do even before you do it. I used the betrayal of Joseph to deliver My people from famine. Your banishment of Moses became his wilderness training. And yes, David did commit adultery with Bathsheba—but he repented of his sin! And thousands have been inspired by his example and found what he found—unending grace. Your deceptions have only served as platforms for My mercy. You are still My servant, Satan. When will you learn? Your feeble attempts to disturb My work only enable My work. Every act you have intended for evil, I have used for good."

Satan began to growl—a throaty, guttural, angry growl. Softly at first, then louder, until the room was filled with a roar that must have quaked the foundations of hell.

But the King was not bothered. "Feeling ill?"

Lucifer lurked around the room, breathing loudly, searching for words to say and a shadow from which to say them. He finally found the words but never the shadow. "Show me, O King of Light, show me one person on the Earth who always does right and obeys your will."

Dare you ask? You know there need be only one perfect one, only one sinless one to die for all the others."

"I know Your plans—and You have failed! No Messiah will come from Your people. There is none who is sinless. Not one." He turned his back to the desk and began naming the children. "Not Moses. Not Abraham. Not Lot. Not Rebekah. Not Elijah…"

The Father stood up from His throne, releasing a wave of holy Light so intense that Lucifer staggered backward and fell. "Those are My children you mock," God's voice boomed. "You think you know much, fallen angel, but you know so little. Your mind dwells in the valley of self. Your eyes see no farther than your own needs."

The King walked over and reached for the book. He turned it toward Lucifer and commanded, "Come, Deceiver, read the name of the One who will call your bluff. Read the name of the One who will storm your gates."

Satan rose slowly off his haunches. Like a wary wolf, he walked a wide circle toward the desk until he stood before the volume and read the word: Immanuel.

"Immanuel?" he muttered to himself, then spoke in a tone of disbelief. "God with us?" For the first time the hooded head turned squarely toward the face of the Father. "No. Not even You would do that. Not even You would go so far."

"You've never believed Me, Satan."

"But Immanuel! The plan is bizarre! You don't know what it's like on Earth! You don't know how dark I've made it. It's putrid. It's evil. It's…"

"It is Mine," proclaimed the King. "And I will reclaim what is Mine. I will become flesh. I will feel what My creatures feel. I will see what they see."

"But what of their sin?"

"I will bring mercy."

"What of their death?"

"I will give life."

Satan stood speechless.

God spoke, "I love My children. Love does not take away the beloved's freedom. But love takes away fear. And Immanuel will leave behind a tribe of fearless children. They will not fear you or your hell."

Satan stepped back at the thought. His retort was childish. "Th-they will too!"

"I will take away all sin. I will take away death. Without sin and without death, you have no power."

Around and around in a circle Satan paced, clenching and unclenching his wiry fingers. When he finally stopped, he asked a question that even I was thinking. 'Why? Why would You do this?"

The Invitation

The Father's voice was deep and soft. "Because I love them."

The two stood facing each other. Neither spoke. The extremes of the universe were before me. God robed in Light, each thread glowing. Satan canopied in evil, the very fabric of his robe seeming to crawl. Peace contrasting panic. Wisdom confronting foolishness. One able to rescue, the other anxious to condemn.

I have reflected much on what happened next. Though I have relived the moment countless times, I'm as stunned as I was at the first. Never in my wildest thoughts did I think my king would do what He did. Had He demanded Satan's departure, who would have questioned? Had He taken Satan's life, who would have grieved? Had He called me to attack, I would have been willing. But God did none of these.

From the circle of Light came His extended hand. From His throne came an honest invitation. "Will you surrender? Will you return to me?"

I do not know the thoughts of Satan. But I believe that for a fleeting second the evil heart softened. The head cocked slightly, as if amazed that such an offer would be made. But then it yanked itself erect. "Where will we battle?" he challenged.

The Father sighed at the dark angel's resistance. "On a hill called Calvary."

"If you make it that far." Satan smirked, spinning and marching out the entryway, and he soared into the heavenlies.

The Father stood motionless for a moment, then turned back to the book. Opening to the final chapter, He slowly read words I had never heard. No sentences. Just words. Saying each, then pausing: JESUS...NAIL... CROSS...TOMB....LIFE.

He motioned toward me, and I responded, kneeling again before Him. Handing me the necklace, he explained, "This vial will contain the essence of Myself; a Seed to be placed in the womb of a young girl. Her name is Mary. She lives among My chosen people. The fruit of the Seed is the Son of God. Take it to her."

"But how will I know her?" I asked.

"Don't worry. You will."

I could not comprehend God's plan, but my understanding was not essential. My obedience was. I lowered my head, and He draped the chain around my neck. Amazingly, the vial was no longer empty. It glowed with Light.

"Jesus. Tell her to call My Son Jesus."

Take My Heart

BILLY GRAHAM
FROM *UNTO THE HILLS*

Our Father and our God, I want my life to count for You and Your Son. Please take my heart and mold it for Your service. Shape it into the servant heart You want it to be. I submit to Your will and Your way for my life. Please give me humility in victory and generosity in defeat. In Jesus' name, Amen.

becauseicare

Because I Care

please take a moment to read the verses written on the next page. Although there are hundreds of verses in the Bible that tell about God's love and His gift of salvation, I chose these from the book of Romans in the New Testament.

I care about what happens to you now, but I care even more about where you will spend eternity. If you have never asked Jesus Christ to be your Savior, please consider inviting Him into your life now.

Many years ago I prayed a simple prayer that went something like this...

Dear Jesus,

I believe you are the Son of God and that you gave your life as a payment for the sins of mankind. I believe you rose from the dead and you are alive today in heaven preparing a place for those who trust in you.

I have not lived my life in a way that honors you. Please forgive me for my sins and come into my life as Savior and Lord. Help me grow in knowledge and obedience to you.

Thank you for forgiving me. Thank you for coming into my life. Thank you for giving me eternal life. Amen.

If you have sincerely asked Jesus Christ to come into your life, He will never leave you or forsake you. Nothing—absolutely nothing—will be able to separate you from His love.

God bless you, dear one. I'll look forward to meeting you one day in heaven.

—Alice Gray

For all have sinned and fall short of the glory of God.

ROMANS 3:23

For the wages of sin is death, but the gift of God
is eternal life in Christ Jesus our Lord.

ROMANS 6:23

But God demonstrates His own love toward us in this:
While we were still sinners, Christ died for us.

ROMANS 5:8

If you confess with your mouth, "Jesus is Lord," and believe
in your heart that God raised him from the dead, you will be saved.
For it is with your heart that you believe and are justified,
and it is with your mouth that you confess and are saved.

ROMANS 10:9–10

Everyone who calls on the name of the Lord will be saved.

ROMANS 10:13

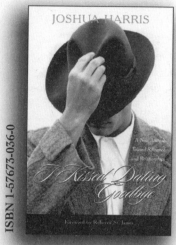

Boy Meets Girl

by Joshua & Shannon Harris

ISBN 1-57673-709-8

I Kissed Dating Goodbye shocked the publishing world in 1995 with its metoric rise to the top of bestseller lists. Teens wanted more than dating "rules"—they wanted an intentional, God-pleasing game plan. In this dynamic sequel, newlyweds Joshua and Shannon Harris deliver an inspiring and practical illustration of how this healthy, joyous alternative to recreational dating—biblical courtship—worked for them. *Boy Meets Girl* helps readers understand how to go about pursuing the possibility of marriage with someone they may be serious about. It's the natural follow-up to the author's blockbuster book on teen dating!

Joshua Harris has a passion to glorify God through preaching and writing. He directs New Attitude Ministries and is in pastoral training at Covenant Life Church in Gaithersburg, Maryland. His new wife, Shannon Harris, contributed to the *I Kissed Dating Goodbye Study Guide* and sings in the contemporary Christian music group *New Attitude*.

Searching for True Love video series

by Joshua Harris

The Searching for True Love video series by Joshua Harris builds on his highly popular conference series and bestselling book *I Kissed Dating Goodbye* to give young adults God's direction as they seek a lifetime love. Available in a three-pack or separately, the videos explore *Love, Purity,* and *Trust* in light of the Bible's perspective. They also help young adults answer vital questions like "How can I honor God in my love life?" and "Is it possible to practice purity in today's society?" Forty-five minutes each.

Three video series	ISBN 1-57673-645-8
Searching for True Love	ISBN 1-57673-634-2
Searching for Trust	ISBN 1-57673-643-1
Searching for Purity	ISBN 1-57673-637-7

Stories for a Teen's Heart

compiled by Alice Gray

A National Bestseller...

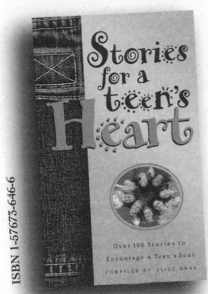

ISBN 1-57673-646-6

Alice Gray has compiled 110 inspirational stories that are touching the hearts of teens everywhere in this popular release in the bestselling Stories for the Heart series. Through an even blend of sometimes humorous, often poignant tales, teens are encouraged in life's journey and reassured that they are not alone on the road to becoming adults. Many popular CBA authors offer valuable insights into the human condition in a manner that is warm and uplifting. *Stories for a Teen's Heart* will revitalize the spirits of young people.

Alice Gray is an inspirational conference speaker and the creator of the bestselling Stories for the Heart book series, now with more than three million copies in print. Alice lives with her husband, Al, in Oregon's high desert country.

Journal for a Teen's Heart

compiled by Alice Gray

As a companion to the bestselling *Stories for a Teen's Heart*, this journal provides an inviting place to record special moments, secret thoughts, and surprising insights. Filled with inspirational thoughts and quotes specific to teen concerns, this diary of a teen's life experience and personal dreams will become a treasured keepsake and a record of growing up. Designed in concealed Y-row binding for easy, lay-flat use, *Journal for a Teen's Heart* is teen-friendly and comfortable for hours of writing, and includes questions to help teens draw out their thoughts and experiences. Repeated use creates a personal resource full of encouraging words about everyday life, friends, family, and faith.

ISBN 1-57673-705-5

Alice Gray is an inspirational conference speaker and the creator of the bestselling Stories for the Heart book series, now with more than three million copies in print. Alice lives with her husband, Al, in Oregon's high desert country.

1 In the Diary series

from *Melody Carlson*

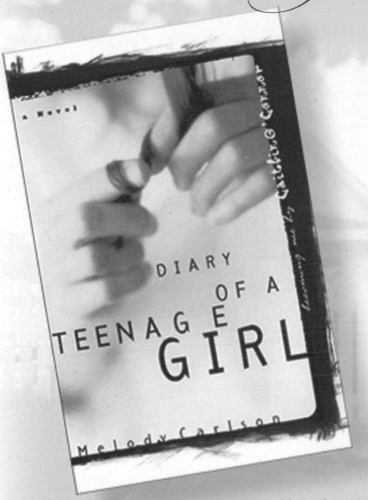

In this compelling journal, sixteen-year-old Caitlin O'Conner explores the conflicts and joys of growing up, including her adventures with boyfriends, peer loyalty, parental conflicts, and spirituality.

ISBN 1-57673-735-7

notes

Send us your stories for
More Stories for a Teen's Heart

We would love to have you submit a story or a quote for our next book for teenagers.

If you don't write the story yourself, please send us as much information as you can about where you found it—things like the name and address of author, name of the book or magazine, date it was published, page number, publisher, and any other information you have. We will credit both you and the original author.

If you write the story yourself, please give us a little information about who you are and what you do.

If you send us something, we will not be able to acknowledge receiving it but promise to contact you if we are going to use it in one of the books in the *Stories for the Heart* series. It is not necessary to send a self-addressed stamped envelope, but be sure to include your name, address, and phone number.

Send stories and quotes to:
Multnomah Publishers, Inc.
Stories for the Heart
P. O. Box 1720
Sisters, Oregon 97759

Acknowledgments

More than a thousand books, magazines, and other sources were researched for this collection as well as a review of hundreds of stories sent by friends and readers of the *Stories for the Heart* collection. A diligent search has been made to trace original ownership, and when necessary, permission to reprint has been obtained. If I have overlooked giving proper credit to anyone, please accept my apologies. If you will contact Multnomah Publishers, Inc., Post Office Box 1720, Sisters, OR 97759, corrections will be made prior to additional printings. Please provide detailed information.

Notes and acknowledgments are listed by story title in the order they appear in each section of the book. For permission to reprint any of the stories please request permission from the original source listed below. Grateful acknowledgment is made to authors, publishers, and agents who granted permission for reprinting these stories.

FORGIVENESS

"Friends to the End" by Cynthia Hamond, S.F.O. © 2000. Used by permission of the author. Cynthia has been in several of the Chicken Soup for the Soul books, magazines, and one of her stories was made for TV. She enjoys speaking and school visits. You may reach her at P.O. Box 488, Monticello, MN 55362, or by e-mail at Candbh@aol.com.

"I Will Always Forgive You" by Joni Eareckson Tada. Excerpted from TELL ME THE PROMISES: A FAMILY COVENANT FOR ETERNITY, Crossway Books, a division of Good News Publishers, Wheaton, IL, © 1996. Used by permission.

"Washed Away" by Janis M. Whipple, editor, Nashville, TN. From Devo'Zine, Nov/Dec 1997. © 1997 by The Upper Room. Used by permission.

"The Room" by Joshua Harris. Taken from I KISSED DATING GOOD-BYE by Joshua Harris © 1997. Used by permission of Multnomah Publishers, Inc.

"The Lovesick Father" by Philip Yancey. Taken from WHAT'S SO

288

AMAZING ABOUT GRACE? by Philip Yancey. Copyright © 1997 by Philip D. Yancey. Used by permission of Zondervan Publishing House.

"An Undeserved Honor" by Jamie Morrison © 2000. Used by permission of the author. Jamie Morrison is a loving husband, father of three, and teaching pastor in upstate New York.

"When I Was a Prodigal Son" by Nanette Thorsen-Snipes © 1999. Used by permission of the author. Her inspirational articles have been published in *Home Life, Breakaway* magazine, *God's Abundance, Chicken Soup for the Soul,* and others. Contact: jsnipes212@aol.com or P.O. Box 1596, Buford, GA 30515.

"Music Lessons" by Katherine Bond © 2000. Used by permission of the author. Katherine Bond is the author of *The Legend of the Valentine* (Zondervan, 2001) and *The Sudden Drown of Knowing* (Brass Weight Press, 2000). "Music Lessons" first appeared in *Focus on the Family Clubhouse.*

"An Unspoken Promise" by Kristi Powers © 1999. Used by permission of the author. Kristi is a stay-at-home mom and loves to share from her heart. She and her husband, Michael, founded StoriesFromMyHeart.Com and can be reached at NoodlesP29@aol.com or 1918 Liberty Lane, Janesville, WI 53545.

VIRTUE

"The Day Lisa Lost" by Michael T. Powers © 1999. Used by permission of the author. Michael and his wife, Kristi, are freelance writers and the founders of StoriesFromMyHeart.Com, an inspirational Internet magazine. Email: Thunder27@aol.com or 1918 Liberty Lane, Janesville, WI 53545.

"The Final I Failed" by Bernice Brooks. Taken from STUFF YOU DON'T HAVE TO PRAY ABOUT by Susie Shellenberger © 1995. Used by permission of Broadman and Holman Publishers, Nashville, TN.

"Choosing Mary" by Daniel Taylor. Taken from LETTERS TO MY CHILDREN by Daniel Taylor © 1989. Used by permission of InterVarsity Press, P.O. Box 1400, Downers Grove, IL 60515. www.ivpress.com

"Toothless Grin" by Sharon Palmer © 1999. Used by permission of the author.

"It Really Didn't Matter" by Charles Colson. Taken from THE BODY by Charles Colson © 1994, Word Publishing, Nashville, Tennessee. Used by permission. All rights reserved.

SHARING YOUR FAITH

LIKE HIS, Crossway Books, a division of Good News Publishers, Wheaton, IL, © 1996. Used by permission.

"The Incredible Power of Words" by Sarah Adams © 2000. Used by permission of the author.

"True Hero of the Titanic" by Moody Adams. Taken from THE TITANIC'S LAST HERO by Moody Adams © 1998. Used by permission of Emerald House Group Inc.

"Thanks for the Bread" by Max Lucado. Taken from IN THE EYE OF THE STORM by Max Lucado © 1991, Word Publishing, Nashville, Tennessee. Used by permission. All rights reserved.

"A Pirate from the House of Prayer" Taken from *Jesus Freaks* by DC Talk and The Voice of the Martyrs (Albury Publishing, Tulsa, OK © 1999). For more information on today's persecuted church, contact The Voice of the Martyrs at www.persecution.com.

"Daughter of the King" by Sheri Rose Shepherd. Taken from LIFE IS NOT A DRESS REHEARSAL by Sheri Rose Shepherd © 2000. Used by permission of Multnomah Publishers, Inc.

MAKING A DIFFERENCE

"Chris's Legacy" by Andy Stanley. Taken from VISIONEERING by Andy Stanley. © 1999. Used by permission of Multnomah Publishers, Inc.

"The Summer That Changed My Life" by Carla Barnhill. From *Campus Life* magazine, Christianity Today, Inc. Copyright © 1997. Used with permission.

"It's Up to You" by Catherine Manceaux. Used by permission of the author. Catherine can be reached by email at wolf130@hotmail.com.

"Bold Faith," adapted from "On Fire in Florida" by Susie Shellenberger, excerpted from *Breakaway* magazine, Vol. 8, No. 11, published by Focus on the Family. Copyright © 1997. All rights reserved. International copyright secured. Used by permission.

"Excuse Me, Is Your Daughter in Trouble?" by Sheri Rose Shepherd. Taken from LIFE IS NOT A DRESS REHEARSAL by Sheri Rose Shepherd © 2000. Used by permission of Multnomah Publishers, Inc.

INSPIRATION

acknowledgments

Merrill © 1994 by Stephen R. Covey, A, Roger Merrill and Rebecca Merrill.

"Third-String Nobody" retold by Duke DuVall. Used by permission of author. Director of Lights of the World Ministries. Web site: lightyourworld-now.com or e-mail: lot@aol.com.

"Life 101" by Phil Callaway. Taken from WHO PUT THE SKUNK IN THE TRUNK © 1999 by Phil Callaway. Used by permission of Multnomah Publishers, Inc.

TRUST AND COURAGE

"Courage Under Fire" by Peter Henderson as told to Sandra P. Aldrich © 1999. Used by permission. Sandra P. Aldrich is a popular speaker and the author/coauthor of 20 books.

"The Rich Family" by Eddie Ogan © 1999. Used be permission of the author.

"The Victor's Crown" retold by Alice Gray. Used by permission.

"Bryon" by Lynn Dixon. © 2000. Used by permission. Lynn Dixon resides in Orangevale, CA, with her husband and young daughter. Prior to having her daughter, she worked with abused and neglected children as a social worker. She enjoys outdoor activities, gardening and writing.

"The Man in Charge" by Betty and Ray Whipps as told to Susan Wales. Taken from A MATCH MADE IN HEAVEN, Volume II © 1999 by Susan Huey-Wales and Ann Williams-Platz. Used by permission of Multnomah Publishers Inc.

"Straight A's" by Helen Heavirland © 1992. Used by permission of author.

"Faith out of Flames" by Cheryl Boersma © 1996. Used by permission of author.

"Spinning out of Control" by Susan Smart © 1998. Used by permission of the author.

"Mandy's Ministry" by Eva Marie Everson © 2000. Used by permission of the author.

CHANGED LIVES

acknowledgments

FAITH

"Table for Two" taken from STILL MORE HOT ILLUSTRATIONS FOR YOUTH TALKS by Wayne Rice. Copyright © 1999 by Youth Specialties, Inc. Used by permission of Zondervan Publishing House.

"Miracles" by Yitta Halberstam and Judith Leventhal. Reprinted with permission. Taken from SMALL MIRACLES II by Yitta Halberstam and Judith Leventhal © 1999. Published by Adams Media Corporation.

"The Story of Her Life" by Kim Claassen. Used by permission of the Luis Palau Evangelistic Association. Copyright © 2000 Luis Palau, P.O. Box 1173, Portland, OR 97207, lpea@palau.org, www.lpea.org.

"Precious Sacrifice" by Billy Graham. Taken from UNTO THE HILLS by Billy Graham, © 1996, Word Publishing, Nashville, Tennessee. Used by permission. All rights reserved.

"A Vital Decision" by Helen Haidle © 1999. Used by permission of the author. Helen Haidle is an award-winning author of over thirty books.

"Mandy's Story" by Luis Palau. Used by permission of the Luis Palau Evangelistic Association. Copyright © 2000 Luis Palau, P.O. Box 1173, Portland, OR 97207 lpea@palau.org, www.lpea.org.

"Safely Home" from the book WHERE ANGELS WALK: *True Stories of Heavenly Visitors* by Joan Wester Anderson. Copyright © 1992 by Joan Wester Anderson. Published by Barton & Brett, Publishers, Inc. Reprinted by permission.

"The Cost" by Philip Yancey. Taken from WHAT'S SO AMAZING ABOUT GRACE by Philip Yancey. Copyright © 1997 by Philip D. Yancey. Used by permission of Zondervan Publishing House.

"The Song" by Nathan S. Abrams. From the April 2000 issue of *Decision* magazine. Used by permission of the author.

"Cosmic Christmas" by Max Lucado. Taken from COSMIC CHRISTMAS by Max Lucado, © 1997, Word Publishing, Nashville, Tennessee. Used by permission. All rights reserved.

"Take My Heart" by Billy Graham. Taken from UNTO THE HILLS by Billy Graham, © 1996, Word Publishing, Nashville, Tennessee. Used by permission. All rights reserved.